A POEM TO READ ALOUD EVERY DAY OF THE YEAR

A POEM
TO READ
ALOUD
EVERY DAY
OF THE YEAR

EDITED BY LIZ ISON

BATSFORD

First published in the United Kingdom in 2023 by

Batsford
43 Great Ormond Street
London
WC1N 3HZ

An imprint of B. T. Batsford Holdings Limited

ISBN 978 1 84994 846 3

A CIP catalogue record for this book
is available from the British Library.

10 9 8 7 6 5

Reproduction by Rival Colour Ltd, UK
Printed by Dream Colour Printing, China.

Illustrations by Ardea-studio/Shutterstock

CONTENTS

Introduction

The poems in this anthology are, in a sense, trapped in inky silence, waiting for you, the reader, to bring them to life. So I encourage you to liberate a poem: turn the pages, find today's date or your birthday or another significant day — and begin a dialogue with a poem.

Poems are, after all, packages of sound, rhythm and meaning, and they need us to animate them, to breathe them. The writer Robert Graves calls a poem 'a living entity' that continues to affect readers with its 'stored magic' long after the end of an author's lifespan. By reading these poems aloud you'll help them find new listeners and readers and so continue their remarkable journeys through time and space. It is readers like you and me who can energize the words by literally transforming them – using the power of mind, body and breath – from the printed page to the spoken word.

From the very earliest age, even in utero, we are drawn to the human voice. Babies and young children particularly love the cadences and rhythms of lullabies and nursery rhymes. Reading stories to children is (or should be) a fundamental part of their first years, whether that is story time in an early years setting or a bedtime book shared as part of the night-time routine, with its opportunity for grown-ups and children to spend quality time together. But it is not just for children. We are never too old to enjoy listening to someone read aloud to us.

It is the same with listening to poetry. Maya Angelou got it right when she wrote, 'it takes the human voice to infuse words with the shades of deeper meaning'. The power of a poem to entertain and stimulate, comfort or console is intensified by reading it aloud. We can recognize our own inner worlds in the words of a poem and find a gateway to our deepest feelings. Reading poems together creates a shared encounter that can live long in the memory. Whether you take on the role of listener or reader, sharing a poem with someone – be that a child or grandchild, parent or grandparent, friend, pupil, partner, lover or stranger – becomes a joint endeavour and will create a special kind of connection.

I strongly believe that reading poetry aloud can help break down the barriers that sometimes exist around it, and can turn fear or puzzlement into a joyful, profound and sometimes transformative experience. Sharing a poem, whether it's with one person or a group of people, whether it is at the family table, at school, in the park, hospital or care home, will open up conversations, improve well-being and build and sustain friendships.

So how do you go about reading poems aloud if you've never done it before or you are a bit out of practice? To get started, you might try reading to yourself in a quiet part of your home. But the best way is to dive in: read to someone you feel comfortable with, or to someone who you think would enjoy it, or who really *needs* it. If you feel a bit self-conscious about reading aloud, don't worry. This is not about a correct way of pronouncing words or creating some kind of performance. Nor is this collection a resource to help organize a poetry recital, or part of a campaign to bring back learning 'by heart' or 'by rote' (although there

is plenty of ideal material in here for these purposes).
This is a book for everyone to enjoy. There is no need
to understand every word and line, or to come up with
a clever comment. Treat the poem as a friend: with
warmth, respect and careful attention. Give the poem
space to breathe by going slowly and giving it a couple
of reads. Then let the words and ideas you've read
and listened to be the springboard for a conversation
between reader and listener.

I hope that reading these poems aloud to family
and friends will help you on your journey through the
changing moods and seasons of the year, and will create
little moments of joy and awe each day.

SOURCES

Maya Angelou, *I Know Why the Caged Bird Sings* (1969)
Robert Graves, *The White Goddess : A Historical Grammar
of Poetic Myth* (1948)

JANUARY

Every Day a Fresh Beginning

The Year

What can be said in New Year rhymes,
That's not been said a thousand times?

The new years come, the old years go,
We know we dream, we dream we know.

We rise up laughing with the light,
We lie down weeping with the night.

We hug the world until it stings,
We curse it then and sigh for wings.

We live, we love, we woo, we wed,
We wreathe our brides, we sheet our dead.

We laugh, we weep, we hope, we fear,
And that's the burden of the year.

Ella Wheeler Wilcox (1850–1919)

January cold desolate

January cold desolate;
February all dripping wet;
March wind ranges;
April changes;
Birds sing in tune
  To flowers of May,
And sunny June
  Brings longest day;
In scorched July
The storm-clouds fly
Lightning-torn;
August bears corn,
September fruit;
In rough October
Earth must disrobe her;
Stars fall and shoot
In keen November;
And night is long
And cold is strong
In bleak December.

Christina Rossetti (1830–1894)

New Every Morning

EXTRACT

Every day is a fresh beginning,
  Every morn is the world made new.
You who are weary of sorrow and sinning,
  Here is a beautiful hope for you,—
  A hope for me and a hope for you.

All the past things are past and over;
  The tasks are done and the tears are shed.
Yesterday's errors let yesterday cover;
  Yesterday's wounds, which smarted and bled,
  Are healed with the healing which night has shed.

Every day is a fresh beginning;
  Listen, my soul, to the glad refrain,
And, spite of old sorrow and older sinning,
  And puzzles forecasted and possible pain,
  Take heart with the day, and begin again.

Susan Coolidge (1835–1905)

Life

Let me but live my life from year to year,
   With forward face and unreluctant soul;
   Not hurrying to, nor turning from, the goal;
Not mourning for the things that disappear
In the dim past, nor holding back in fear
   From what the future veils; but with a whole
   And happy heart, that pays its toll
To Youth and Age, and travels on with cheer.

So let the way wind up the hill or down,
   O'er rough or smooth, the journey will be joy:
   Still seeking what I sought when but a boy,
New friendship, high adventure, and a crown,
My heart will keep the courage of the quest,
And hope the road's last turn will be the best.

Henry Van Dyke (1852–1933)

Ode: We are the music-makers

EXTRACT

We are the music-makers,
    And we are the dreamers of dreams,
Wandering by lone sea-breakers
    And sitting by desolate streams;—
World-losers and world-forsakers,
    On whom the pale moon gleams:
Yet we are the movers and shakers
    Of the world for ever, it seems.

With wonderful deathless ditties
We build up the world's great cities,
    And out of a fabulous story
    We fashion an empire's glory:
One man with a dream, at pleasure,
    Shall go forth and conquer a crown;
And three with a new song's measure
    Can trample an empire down.

We, in the ages lying
    In the buried past of the earth,
Built Nineveh with our sighing,
    And Babel itself with our mirth;
And o'erthrew them with prophesying
    To the old of the new world's worth;
For each age is a dream that is dying,
    Or one that is coming to birth.

Arthur O'Shaughnessy (1844–1881)

January

EXTRACT

No birds sing, but the starling chaps his bill
   And chatters mockingly; the newborn lambs
Within their strawbuilt fold beneath the hill
   Answer with plaintive cry their bleating dams.

Their voices melt in welcome dreams of spring,
   Green grass and leafy trees and sunny skies:
My fancy decks the woods, the thrushes sing,
   Meadows are gay, bees hum and scents arise.

Robert Bridges (1844–1930)

A Book of Verses

FROM *THE RUBÁIYÁT OF OMAR KHAYYAM*

A Book of Verses underneath the Bough,
A Jug of Wine, a Loaf of Bread—and Thou
   Beside me singing in the Wilderness—
  Oh, Wilderness were Paradise enow!

Ah, make the most of what we yet may spend,
Before we too into the Dust descend;
   Dust into Dust, and under Dust to lie,
  Sans Wine, sans Song, sans Singer, and—sans End!

Omar Khayyam (1048–1131)
Translated from the Persian by Edward FitzGerald (1809–1883)

Snow-flakes

Out of the bosom of the Air,
  Out of the cloud-folds of her garments shaken,
Over the woodlands brown and bare,
  Over the harvest-fields forsaken,
    Silent, and soft, and slow
    Descends the snow.

Even as our cloudy fancies take
  Suddenly shape in some divine expression,
Even as the troubled heart doth make
  In the white countenance confession,
    The troubled sky reveals
    The grief it feels.

This is the poem of the air,
  Slowly in silent syllables recorded;
This is the secret of despair,
  Long in its cloudy bosom hoarded,
    Now whispered and revealed
    To wood and field.

Henry Wadsworth Longfellow (1807–1882)

Snow in the Suburbs

Every branch big with it,
   Bent every twig with it;
 Every fork like a white web-foot;
 Every street and pavement mute:
Some flakes have lost their way, and grope back upward
   when
Meeting those meandering down they turn and descend
   again.
 The palings are glued together like a wall,
 And there is no waft of wind with the fleecy fall.

A sparrow enters the tree,
   Whereon immediately
 A snow-lump thrice his own slight size
 Descends on him and showers his head and eye
   And overturns him,
   And near inurns him,
 And lights on a nether twig, when its brush
Starts off a volley of other lodging lumps with a rush.

The steps are a blanched slope,
   Up which, with feeble hope,
 A black cat comes, wide-eyed and thin;
 And we take him in.

Thomas Hardy (1840–1928)

Out in the Dark

Out in the dark over the snow
The fallow fawns invisible go
With the fallow doe;
And the winds blow
Fast as the stars are slow.

Stealthily the dark haunts round
And, when the lamp goes, without sound
At a swifter bound
Than the swiftest hound,
Arrives, and all else is drowned;

And I and star and wind and deer,
Are in the dark together,—near,
Yet far,—and fear
Drums on my ear
In that sage company drear.

How weak and little is the light,
All the universe of sight,
Love and delight,
Before the might,
If you love it not, of night.

Edward Thomas (1878–1917)

Shadow March

All round the house is the jet-black night;
  It stares through the window-pane;
It crawls in the corners, hiding from the light,
  And it moves with the moving flame.

Now my little heart goes a-beating like a drum,
  With the breath of the Bogie in my hair;
And all round the candle the crooked shadows come
  And go marching along up the stair.

The shadow of the balusters, the shadow of the lamp,
  The shadow of the child that goes to bed—
All the wicked shadows coming, tramp, tramp, tramp,
  With the black night overhead.

Robert Louis Stevenson (1850–1894)

To You

EXTRACT

Whoever you are, I fear you are walking the walks of
  dreams,
I fear these supposed realities are to melt from under
  your feet and hands,
Even now your features, joys, speech, house, trade,
  manners, troubles, follies, costume, crimes, dissipate
  away from you,
Your true soul and body appear before me,
They stand forth out of affairs, out of commerce, shops,
  work, farms, clothes, the house, buying, selling, eating,
  drinking, suffering, dying.

Whoever you are, now I place my hand upon you, that
  you be my poem,
I whisper with my lips close to your ear.

Walt Whitman (1819–1892)

Songs

SECOND AND THIRD SONGS FROM *THE GYPSIES METAMORPHOSED*

The faery beam upon you,
  The stars to glister on you;
    A moon of light,
    In the noon of night,
Till the fire-drake hath o'ergone you!
The wheel of fortune guide you,
The boy with the bow beside you
    Run aye in the way,
    Till the bird of the day,
And the luckier lot betide you!
     * * * *

To the old, long life and treasure;
To the young, all health and pleasure;
    To the fair, their face
    With eternal grace;
And the soul to be loved at leisure.
To the witty, all clear mirrors,
To the foolish their dark errors;
    To the loving sprite,
    A secure delight:
To the jealous his own false terrors.

Ben Jonson (1572–1637)

Invitation to Love

Come when the nights are bright with stars
  Or come when the moon is mellow;
Come when the sun his golden bars
  Drops on the hay-field yellow.
Come in the twilight soft and gray,
Come in the night or come in the day,
Come, O love, whene'er you may,
  And you are welcome, welcome.

You are sweet, O Love, dear Love,
You are soft as the nesting dove.
Come to my heart and bring it to rest
As the bird flies home to its welcome nest.

Come when my heart is full of grief
  Or when my heart is merry;
Come with the falling of the leaf
  Or with the redd'ning cherry.
Come when the year's first blossom blows,
Come when the summer gleams and glows,
Come with the winter's drifting snows,
  And you are welcome, welcome.

Paul Laurence Dunbar (1872–1906)

Love is not all

Love is not all: it is not meat nor drink
Nor slumber nor a roof against the rain,
Nor yet a floating spar to men that sink
And rise and sink and rise and sink again;
Love can not fill the thickened lung with breath,
Nor clean the blood, nor set the fractured bone;
Yet many a man is making friends with death
Even as I speak, for lack of love alone.
It well may be that in a difficult hour,
Pinned down by pain and moaning for release,
Or nagged by want past resolution's power,
I might be driven to sell your love for peace,
Or trade the memory of this night for food.
It well may be. I do not think I would.

Edna St. Vincent Millay (1892–1950)

Endure Hardness

A cold wind stirs the blackthorn
  To burgeon and to blow,
Besprinkling half-green hedges
  With flakes and sprays of snow.

Through coldness and through keenness,
  Dear hearts, take comfort so:
Somewhere or other doubtless
  These make the blackthorn blow.

Christina Rossetti (1830–1894)

The Sea-Limits

EXTRACT

Listen alone beside the sea,
  Listen alone among the woods;
  Those voices of twin solitudes
Shall have one sound alike to thee:
  Hark where the murmurs of thronged men
  Surge and sink back and surge again,—
Still the one voice of wave and tree.

Gather a shell from the strown beach
  And listen at its lips: they sigh
  The same desire and mystery,
The echo of the whole sea's speech
  And all mankind is thus at heart
  Not anything but what thou art:
And Earth, Sea, Man, are all in each.

Dante Gabriel Rossetti (1828–1882)

The Sound of the Sea

The sea awoke at midnight from its sleep,
   And round the pebbly beaches far and wide
   I heard the first wave of the rising tide
   Rush onward with uninterrupted sweep;
A voice out of the silence of the deep,
   A sound mysteriously multiplied
   As of a cataract from the mountain's side,
   Or roar of winds upon a wooded steep.
So comes to us at times, from the unknown
   And inaccessible solitudes of being,
   The rushing of the sea-tides of the soul;
And inspirations, that we deem our own,
   Are some divine of foreshadowing and foreseeing
   Of things beyond our reason or control.

Henry Wadsworth Longfellow (1807–1882)

Speak Gently

EXTRACT

Speak gently! it is better far
  To rule by love than fear:
Speak gently! let no harsh words mar
  The good we might do here.

Speak gently: 'tis a little thing
  Dropped in the heart's deep well;
The good, the joy, which it may bring,
  Eternity shall tell.

George Washington Langford

The Lesson

My cot was down by a cypress grove,
  And I sat by my window the whole night long,
And heard well up from the deep dark wood
  A mocking-bird's passionate song.

And I thought of myself so sad and lone,
  And my life's cold winter that knew no spring;
Of my mind so weary and sick and wild,
  Of my heart too sad to sing.

But e'en as I listened the mock-bird's song,
  A thought stole into my saddened heart,
And I said, 'I can cheer some other soul
  By a carol's simple art.'

For oft from the darkness of hearts and lives
  Come songs that brim with joy and light,
As out of the gloom of the cypress grove
  The mocking-bird sings at night.

So I sang a lay for a brother's ear
  In a strain to soothe his bleeding heart,
And he smiled at the sound of my voice and lyre,
  Though mine was a feeble art.

But at his smile I smiled in turn,
  And into my soul there came a ray:
In trying to soothe another's woes
  Mine own had passed away.

Paul Laurence Dunbar (1872–1906)

Solitude

Laugh, and the world laughs with you;
  Weep, and you weep alone;
For the sad old earth must borrow its mirth,
  But has trouble enough of its own.
Sing, and the hills will answer;
  Sigh, it is lost on the air;
The echoes bound to a joyful sound,
  But shrink from voicing care.

Rejoice, and men will seek you;
  Grieve, and they turn and go;
They want full measure of all your pleasure,
  But they do not need your woe.
Be glad, and your friends are many;
  Be sad, and you lose them all,—
There are none to decline your nectared wine,
  But alone you must drink life's gall.

Feast, and your halls are crowded;
  Fast, and the world goes by.
Succeed and give, and it helps you live,
  But no man can help you die.
There is room in the halls of pleasure
  For a large and lordly train,
But one by one we must all file on
  Through the narrow aisles of pain.

Ella Wheeler Wilcox (1850–1919)

Where My Books Go

All the words that I utter,
    And all the words that I write,
Must spread out their wings untiring,
    And never rest in their flight,
Till they come where your sad, sad heart is,
    And sing to you in the night,
Beyond where the waters are moving,
    Storm-darken'd or starry bright.

W.B. Yeats (1865–1939)

Romance

To clasp you now and feel your head close-pressed,
Scented and warm against my beating breast;

To whisper soft and quivering your name,
And drink the passion burning in your frame;

To lie at full length, taut, with cheek to cheek,
And tease your mouth with kisses till you speak

Love words, mad words, dream words, sweet senseless
  words,
Melodious like notes of mating birds;

To hear you ask if I shall love always,
And myself answer: Till the end of days;

To feel your easeful sigh of happiness
When on your trembling lips I murmur: Yes;

It is so sweet. We know it is not true.
What matters it? The night must shed her dew.

We know it is not true, but it is sweet—
The poem with this music is complete.

Claude McKay (1889–1948)

The Lover's Appeal

And wilt thou leave me thus?
Say nay, say nay, for shame,
To save thee from the blame
Of all my grief and grame.
And wilt thou leave me thus?
  Say nay, say nay!

And wilt thou leave me thus,
That hath loved thee so long
In wealth and woe among?
And is thy heart so strong
As for to leave me thus?
  Say nay, say nay.

And wilt thou leave me thus,
That hath given thee my heart
Never for to depart
Neither for pain nor smart?
And wilt thou leave me thus?
  Say nay, say nay.

And wilt thou leave me thus,
And have no more pity
Of him that loveth thee?
Alas! thy cruelty!
And wilt thou leave me thus?
  Say nay, say nay!

Thomas Wyatt (1503–1542)

Up in the Morning Early

Cauld blaws the wind frae east to west,
The drift is driving sairly;
Sae loud and shrill's I hear the blast,
I'm sure it's winter fairly.

Up in the morning's no for me,
Up in the morning early;
When a' the hills are cover'd wi' snaw,
I'm sure its winter fairly.

The birds sit chittering in the thorn,
A' day they fare but sparely;
And lang's the night frae e'en to morn,
I'm sure it's winter fairly.

Up in the morning's no for me,
Up in the morning early;
When a' the hills are cover'd wi' snaw,
I'm sure its winter fairly.

Robert Burns (1759–1796)

Armenian Lullaby

EXTRACT

If thou wilt close thy drowsy eyes,
  My mulberry one, my golden son,
The rose shall sing thee lullabies,
  My pretty cosset lambkin!
And thou shalt swing in an almond-tree,
With a flood of moonbeams rocking thee,—
A silver boat in a golden sea,—
  My velvet love, my nestling dove,
  My own pomegranate-blossom!

And when the morn wakes up to see
  My apple-bright, my soul's delight,
The partridge shall come calling thee,
  My jar of milk-and-honey!
Yes, thou shalt know what mystery lies
In the amethyst deep of the curtained skies,
If thou wilt fold thy onyx eyes,
  You wakeful one, you naughty son,
  You chirping little sparrow!

Eugene Field (1850–1895)

The Tablecloth

A tablecloth,
A white, coarse linen weave,
A dead thing, so it seems.
Its threads are gently rent
In places, as in dreams,
When falling into pits
We wake in unbelief.

So frays this weft.
My father's mother made
The cloth in quiet days.
What patient thoughts she wove
Around this loom, narrow
Village ways, important
Hours underlined her shade.

Now, when I touch
This fragile web, and spread
It with our wine and bread,
And watch it slowly die,
I grieve not for its breach
But for the broken peace,
The rootlessness, our dread.

Lotte Kramer (b.1923)

Dreams

Here we are all, by day; by night we're hurl'd
By dreams, each one into a several world.

Robert Herrick (1591–1674)

January, 1795

EXTRACT

Pavement slipp'ry, people sneezing,
Lords in ermine, beggars freezing;
Titled gluttons dainties carving,
Genius in a garret starving.

Lofty mansions, warm and spacious;
Courtiers cringing and voracious;
Misers scarce the wretched heeding;
Gallant soldiers fighting, bleeding.

Poets, painters, and musicians;
Lawyers, doctors, politicians:
Pamphlets, newspapers, and odes,
Seeking fame by diff'rent roads.

Mary Robinson (1758–1800)

The Fallow Deer at the Lonely House

One without looks in to-night
　　Through the curtain chink
From the sheet of glistening white;
One without looks in tonight
　　As we sit and think
　　By the fender-brink.

We do not discern those eyes
　　Watching in the snow;
Lit by lamps of rosy dyes
We do not discern those eyes
　　Wondering, aglow
　　Four footed, tiptoe.

Thomas Hardy (1840–1928)

Let There Be Peace

Let there be peace
So frowns fly away like albatross
And skeletons foxtrot from cupboards,
So war correspondents become travel show presenters
And magpies bring back lost property,
Children, engagement rings, broken things.

Let there be peace
So storms can go out to sea to be
Angry and return to me calm,
So the broken can rise up and dance in the hospitals.
Let the aged Ethiopian man in the grey block of flats
Peer through his window and see Addis before him,
So his thrilled outstretched arms become frames
For his dreams.

Let there be peace
Let tears evaporate to form clouds, cleanse themselves
And fall into reservoirs of drinking water.
Let harsh memories burst into fireworks that melt
In the dark pupils of a child's eyes
And disappear like shoals of silver darting fish,
And let the waves reach the shore with a
Shhhhhhhhhhhhhhh Shhhhhhhhhhhhhhhh
  Shhhhhhhhhhhhhhhh

Lemn Sissay (b.1967)

FEBRUARY

Fairy Lands of Fabled Lore

London Snow

EXTRACT

When men were all asleep the snow came flying,
In large white flakes falling on the city brown,
Stealthily and perpetually settling and loosely lying,
    Hushing the latest traffic of the drowsy town;
Deadening, muffling, stifling its murmurs failing;
Lazily and incessantly floating down and down:
    Silently sifting and veiling road, roof and railing;
Hiding difference, making unevenness even,
Into angles and crevices softly drifting and sailing.
    All night it fell, and when full inches seven
It lay in the depth of its uncompacted lightness,
The clouds blew off from a high and frosty heaven;
    And all woke earlier for the unaccustomed brightness
Of the winter dawning, the strange unheavenly glare:
The eye marvelled—marvelled at the dazzling whiteness;
    The ear hearkened to the stillness of the solemn air;
No sound of wheel rumbling nor of foot falling,
And the busy morning cries came thin and spare.
    Then boys I heard, as they went to school, calling,
They gathered up the crystal manna to freeze
Their tongues with tasting, their hands with snowballing;
    Or rioted in a drift, plunging up to the knees;
Or peering up from under the white-mossed wonder,
'O look at the trees!' they cried, 'O look at the trees!'

Robert Bridges (1844–1930)

Just Whistle a Bit

EXTRACT

Just whistle a bit, if the night be drear
  And the stars refuse to shine:
And a gleam that mocks the starlight clear
  Within you glows benign.

Till the dearth of light in the glooming skies
Is lost to the sight of your soul-lit eyes.
What matters the absence of moon or star?
The light within is the best by far.

* * * *

Just whistle a bit, if your heart be sore;
  'Tis a wonderful balm for pain.
Just pipe some old melody o'er and o'er
  Till it soothes like summer rain.

And perhaps 't would be best in a later day,
When Death comes stalking down the way,
To knock at your bosom and see if you're fit,
Then, as you wait calmly, just whistle a bit.

Paul Laurence Dunbar (1872–1906)

Invictus

Out of the night that covers me,
  Black as the pit from pole to pole,
I thank whatever gods may be
  For my unconquerable soul.

In the fell clutch of circumstance
  I have not winced nor cried aloud.
Under the bludgeonings of chance
  My head is bloody, but unbowed.

Beyond this place of wrath and tears
  Looms but the Horror of the shade,
And yet the menace of the years
  Finds and shall find me unafraid.

It matters not how strait the gate,
  How charged with punishments the scroll.
I am the master of my fate:
  I am the captain of my soul.

William Ernest Henley (1849–1903)

The night is darkening round me

The night is darkening round me,
  The wild winds coldly blow;
But a tyrant spell has bound me
  And I cannot, cannot go.

The giant trees are bending
  Their bare boughs weighed with snow.
The storm is fast descending,
  And yet I cannot go.

Clouds beyond clouds above me,
  Wastes beyond wastes below;
But nothing drear can move me—
  I will not, cannot go.

Emily Brontë (1818–1848)

Come, read to me some poem

EXTRACTS FROM *THE DAY IS DONE*

Come, read to me some poem,
  Some simple and heartfelt lay,
That shall soothe this restless feeling,
  And banish the thoughts of day.

Not from the grand old masters,
  Not from the bards sublime,
Whose distant footsteps echo
  Through the corridors of Time.

Read from some humbler poet,
  Whose songs gushed from his heart,
As showers from the clouds of summer,
  Or tears from the eyelids start;

Such songs have power to quiet
  The restless pulse of care,
And come like the benediction
  That follows after prayer.

Then read from the treasured volume
  The poem of thy choice,
And lend to the rhyme of the poet
  The beauty of thy voice.

Henry Wadsworth Longfellow (1807–1882)

All the world's a stage

FROM *AS YOU LIKE IT*, ACT II, SCENE VII

All the world's a stage,
And all the men and women merely players:
They have their exits and their entrances;
And one man in his time plays many parts,
His acts being seven ages. At first the infant,
Mewling and puking in the nurse's arms.
And then the whining school-boy, with his satchel
And shining morning face, creeping like snail
Unwillingly to school. And then the lover,
Sighing like furnace, with a woeful ballad
Made to his mistress' eyebrow. Then a soldier,
Full of strange oaths and bearded like the pard,
Jealous in honour, sudden and quick in quarrel,
Seeking the bubble reputation
Even in the cannon's mouth. And then the justice,
In fair round belly with good capon lined,
With eyes severe and beard of formal cut,
Full of wise saws and modern instances;
And so he plays his part. The sixth age shifts
Into the lean and slipper'd pantaloon,
With spectacles on nose and pouch on side,
His youthful hose, well saved, a world too wide
For his shrunk shank; and his big manly voice,
Turning again toward childish treble, pipes
And whistles in his sound. Last scene of all,
That ends this strange eventful history,
Is second childishness and mere oblivion,
Sans teeth, sans eyes, sans taste, sans everything.

William Shakespeare (1564–1616)

How Do I Love Thee?

How do I love thee? Let me count the ways.
I love thee to the depth and breadth and height
My soul can reach, when feeling out of sight
For the ends of Being and ideal Grace.
I love thee to the level of every day's
Most quiet need, by sun and candlelight.
I love thee freely, as men strive for Right.
I love thee purely, as they turn from Praise.
I love thee with the passion put to use
In my old griefs, and with my childhood's faith.
I love thee with a love I seemed to lose
With my lost saints. I love thee with the breath,
Smiles, tears, of all my life!—and, if God choose,
I shall but love thee better after death.

Elizabeth Barrett Browning (1806–1861)

Summum Bonum

All the breath and the bloom of the year in the bag of
  one bee:
All the wonder and wealth of the mine in the heart of
  one gem:
In the core of one pearl all the shade and the shine of the
  sea:
Breath and bloom, shade and shine,—wonder, wealth,
  and—how far above them—
    Truth, that's brighter than gem,
    Trust, that's purer than pearl,—
Brightest truth, purest trust in the universe—all were for
  me
    In the kiss of one girl.

Robert Browning (1812–1889)

Now Sleeps the Crimson Petal

FROM *THE PRINCESS*

Now sleeps the crimson petal, now the white;
Nor waves the cypress in the palace walk;
Nor winks the gold fin in the porphyry font.
The firefly wakens: waken thou with me.

Now droops the milkwhite peacock like a ghost,
And like a ghost she glimmers on to me.

Now lies the Earth all Danaë to the stars,
And all thy heart lies open unto me.

Now slides the silent meteor on, and leaves
A shining furrow, as thy thoughts in me.

Now folds the lily all her sweetness up,
And slips into the bosom of the lake:
So fold thyself, my dearest, thou, and slip
Into my bosom and be lost in me.

Alfred, Lord Tennyson (1809–1892)

She Walks in Beauty

She walks in Beauty, like the night
  Of cloudless climes and starry skies;
And all that's best of dark and bright
  Meet in her aspect and her eyes;
Thus mellowed to that tender light
  Which Heaven to gaudy day denies.

One shade the more, one ray the less,
  Had half impaired the nameless grace
Which waves in every raven tress,
  Or softly lightens o'er her face;
Where thoughts serenely sweet express,
  How pure, how dear their dwelling-place.

And on that cheek, and o'er that brow,
  So soft, so calm, yet eloquent,
The smiles that win, the tints that glow,
  But tell of days in goodness spent,
A mind at peace with all below,
  A heart whose love is innocent!

Lord Byron (1788–1824)

Breakfast

A dinner party, coffee, tea,
Sandwich, or supper, all may be
In their way pleasant. But to me
Not one of these deserves the praise
That welcomer of new-born days,
A *breakfast*, merits; ever giving
Cheerful notice we are living
Another day refreshed by sleep,
When its festival we keep.
Now although I would not slight
Those kindly words we use 'Good night',
Yet parting words are words of sorrow,
And may not vie with sweet 'Good Morrow',
With which again our friends we greet,
When in the breakfast-room we meet,
At the social table round,
Listening to the lively sound

Of those notes which never tire,
Of urn, or kettle on the fire.
Sleepy Robert never hears
Or urn, or kettle; he appears
When all have finished, one by one
Dropping off, and breakfast done.
Yet has he too his own pleasure,
His breakfast hour's his hour of leisure;
And, left alone, he reads or muses,
Or else in idle mood he uses
To sit and watch the venturous fly,
Where the sugar's piled high,
Clambering o'er the lumps so white,
Rocky cliffs of sweet delight.

Mary Lamb (1764–1847)

Friendship

Oh, the comfort, the inexpressible comfort of feeling
  safe with a person,
Having neither to weight thoughts,
Nor measure words—but pouring them
All right out—just as they are—
Chaff and grain together—
Certain that a faithful hand will
Take and sift them—
Keep what is worth keeping—
And with the breath of kindness
Blow the rest away.

Dinah Maria Craik (1826–1887)

If I can stop one heart from breaking

If I can stop one heart from breaking
I shall not live in vain;
If I can ease one life the aching,
Or cool one pain,
Or help one fainting robin
Unto his nest again,
I shall not live in vain.

Emily Dickinson (1830–1886)

Sonnet for the 14th of February

No popular respect will I omit
To do thee honor on this happy day,
When every loyal lover tasks his wit
His simple truth in studious rhymes to pay,
And to his mistress dear his hopes convey.
Rather thou knowest I would still outrun
All calendars with Love's,—whose date alway
Thy bright eyes govern better than the Sun,—
For with thy favor was my life begun;
And still I reckon on from smiles to smiles,
And not by summers, for I thrive on none
But those thy cheerful countenance complies:
Oh! if it be to choose and call thee mine,
Love, thou art every day my Valentine.

Thomas Hood (1799–1845)

I wish I could remember that first day

FROM *MONNA INNOMINATA 2*

I wish I could remember that first day,
   First hour, first moment of your meeting me,
   If bright or dim the season, it might be
Summer or Winter for aught I can say;
So unrecorded did it slip away,
   So blind was I to see and to foresee,
   So dull to mark the budding of my tree
That would not blossom yet for many a May.
If only I could recollect it, such
   A day of days! I let it come and go
   As traceless as a thaw of bygone snow;
It seemed to mean so little, meant so much;
If only now I could recall that touch,
   First touch of hand in hand—Did one but know!

Christina Rossetti (1830–1894)

Stanzas

O, come to me in dreams, my love!
  I will not ask a dearer bliss;
Come with the starry beams, my love,
  And press mine eyelids with thy kiss.

'Twas thus, as ancient fables tell,
  Love visited a Grecian maid,
Till she disturbed the sacred spell,
  And woke to find her hopes betrayed.

But gentle sleep shall veil my sight,
  And Psyche's lamp shall darkling be,
When, in the visions of the night,
  Thou dost renew thy vows to me.

Then come to me in dreams, my love,
  I will not ask a dearer bliss;
Come with the starry beams, my love,
  And press mine eyelids with thy kiss.

Mary Shelley (1797–1851)

A Widow Bird

SONG FROM *CHARLES THE FIRST*

A widow bird sate mourning for her Love
  Upon a wintry bough;
The frozen wind crept on above
  The freezing stream below.

There was no leaf upon the forest bare,
  No flower upon the ground,
And little motion in the air
  Except the mill-wheel's sound.

Percy Bysshe Shelley (1792–1822)

Kubla Khan

OR, A VISION IN A DREAM. A FRAGMENT

In Xanadu did Kubla Khan
A stately pleasure-dome decree:
Where Alph, the sacred river, ran
Through caverns measureless to man
   Down to a sunless sea.
So twice five miles of fertile ground
With walls and towers were girdled round:
And there were gardens bright with sinuous rills,
Where blossomed many an incense-bearing tree;
And here were forests ancient as the hills,
Enfolding sunny spots of greenery.

But oh! that deep romantic chasm which slanted
Down the green hill athwart a cedarn cover!
A savage place! as holy and enchanted
As e'er beneath a waning moon was haunted
By woman wailing for her demon-lover!
And from this chasm, with ceaseless turmoil seething,
As if this earth in fast thick pants were breathing,
A mighty fountain momently was forced:
Amid whose swift half-intermitted burst
Huge fragments vaulted like rebounding hail,
Or chaffy grain beneath the thresher's flail:
And mid these dancing rocks at once and ever
It flung up momently the sacred river.
Five miles meandering with a mazy motion
Through wood and dale the sacred river ran,
Then reached the caverns measureless to man,
And sank in tumult to a lifeless ocean:

And 'mid this tumult Kubla heard from far
Ancestral voices prophesying war!
  The shadow of the dome of pleasure
  Floated midway on the waves;
  Where was heard the mingled measure
  From the fountain and the caves.
It was a miracle of rare device,
A sunny pleasure-dome with caves of ice!

  A damsel with a dulcimer
  In a vision once I saw:
  It was an Abyssinian maid
  And on her dulcimer she played,
  Singing of Mount Abora.
  Could I revive within me
  Her symphony and song,
  To such a deep delight 'twould win me,
That with music loud and long,
I would build that dome in air,
That sunny dome! those caves of ice!
And all who heard should see them there,
And all should cry, Beware! Beware!
His flashing eyes, his floating hair!
Weave a circle round him thrice,
And close your eyes with holy dread
For he on honey-dew hath fed,
And drunk the milk of Paradise.

Samuel Taylor Coleridge (1772–1834)

Eldorado

Gaily bedight,
 A gallant knight,
In sunshine and in shadow,
 Had journeyed long,
 Singing a song,
In search of Eldorado

But he grew old—
 This knight so bold—
And o'er his heart a shadow—
 Fell as he found
 No spot of ground
That looked like Eldorado.

And, as his strength
 Failed him at length,
He met a pilgrim shadow—
 'Shadow,' said he,
 'Where can it be—
This land of Eldorado?'

'Over the Mountains
 Of the Moon,
Down the Valley of the Shadow,
 Ride, boldly ride,'
 The shade replied,—
'If you seek for Eldorado.'

Edgar Allan Poe (1809–1849)

Once more unto the breach, dear friends

FROM *HENRY V*, ACT III, SCENE I

Once more unto the breach, dear friends, once more;
Or close the wall up with our English dead.
In peace there's nothing so becomes a man
As modest stillness and humility:
But when the blast of war blows in our ears,
Then imitate the action of the tiger;
Stiffen the sinews, summon up the blood,
Disguise fair nature with hard-favour'd rage;
Then lend the eye a terrible aspect;
Let pry through the portage of the head
Like the brass cannon; let the brow o'erwhelm it
As fearfully as doth a galled rock
O'erhang and jutty his confounded base,
Swill'd with the wild and wasteful ocean.
Now set the teeth and stretch the nostril wide,
Hold hard the breath and bend up every spirit
To his full height. On, on, you noblest English.

William Shakespeare (1564–1616)

Magpies in Picardy

The magpies in Picardy
Are more than I can tell.
They flicker down the dusty roads
And cast a magic spell
On the men who march through Picardy,
Through Picardy to hell.

(The blackbird flies with panic,
The swallow goes like light,
The finches move like ladies,
The owl floats by at night;
But the great and flashing magpie
He flies as artists might.)

A magpie in Picardy
Told me secret things—
Of the music in white feathers,
And the sunlight that sings
And dances in deep shadows—
He told me with his wings.

(The hawk is cruel and rigid,
He watches from a height;
The rook is slow and sombre,
The robin loves to fight;
But the great and flashing magpie
He flies as lovers might.)

He told me that in Picardy,
An age ago or more,
While all his fathers still were eggs,
These dusty highways bore
Brown, singing soldiers marching out
Through Picardy to war.

He said that still through chaos
Works on the ancient plan,
And two things have altered not
Since first the world began—
The beauty of the wild green earth
And the bravery of man.

(For the sparrow flies unthinking
And quarrels in his flight;
The heron trails his legs behind,
The lark goes out of sight;
But the great and flashing magpie
He flies as poets might.)

T. P. Cameron Wilson (1888–1918)

Entirely

If we could get the hang of it entirely
    It would take too long;
All we know is the splash of words in passing
    And falling twigs of song,
And when we try to eavesdrop on the great
    Presences it is rarely
That by a stroke of luck we can appropriate
    Even a phrase entirely.

If we could find our happiness entirely
    In somebody else's arms
We should not fear the spears of the spring nor the city's
    Yammering fire alarms
But, as it is, the spears each year go through
    Our flesh and almost hourly
Bell or siren banishes the blue
    Eyes of Love entirely.

And if the world were black or white entirely
    And all the charts were plain
Instead of a mad weir of tigerish waters,
    A prism of delight and pain,
We might be surer where we wished to go
    Or again we might be merely
Bored but in the brute reality there is no
    Road that is right entirely.

Louis MacNeice (1907–1963)

The Coming of Good Luck

So Good-Luck came, and on my roof did light,
Like noiseless snow, or as the dew of night;
Not all at once, but gently,—as the trees
Are by the sun-beams, tickled by degrees.

Robert Herrick (1591–1674)

All the Hemispheres

Leave the familiar for a while.
Let your senses and bodies stretch out

Like a welcomed season
Onto the meadows and shores and hills.

Open up to the Roof.
Make a new water-mark on your excitement
And love.

Like a blooming night flower,
Bestow your vital fragrance of happiness
And giving
Upon our intimate assembly.

Change rooms in your mind for a day.

All the hemispheres in existence
Lie beside an equator
In your heart.

Greet Yourself
In your thousand other forms
As you mount the hidden tide and travel
Back home.

All the hemispheres in heaven
Are sitting around a fire
Chatting

While stitching themselves together
Into the Great Circle inside of
You.

Hafiz (c.1320–1389)
Translated from the Persian by Daniel Ladinsky (b.1948)

The Way

Friend, I have lost the way.
The way leads on.
Is there another way?
The way is one.
I must retrace the track.
It's lost and gone.
Back, I must travel back!
None goes there, none.
Then I'll make here my place,
(The road leads on),
Stand still and set my face,
(The road leaps on),
Stay here, for ever stay.
None stays here, none.
I cannot find the way.
The way leads on.
Oh places I have passed!
That journey's done.
And what will come at last?
The road leads on.

Edwin Muir (1887–1959)

A Poet's Atlantis

Away! Away! We will sail the sea,
   To find some sweet and flowery isle,
In the waste of waters, far and free
   From worldly grief and worldling's guile;
Where the earth blooms ever fair beneath,
   The smile of a genial sky above,
There no more the bitter sigh to breathe,
   But in bowers of bliss to live and love!

O! May our barque, with favouring gale,
   A haven reach on such a shore,
Like the Edens traced in eastern tale,
   Or the fairy lands of fabled lore;
Where life would be one delicious dream
   Of the after bliss we hope above,
Reflecting, like some stainless stream,
   The hues of heaven, the light of love!

Without regard, and without regret,
   We'll quit all we have valued here,
Our wrongs forgive, and our woes forget,
   In the joy and peace of another sphere;
Where the morning breaks with an angel's smile,
   And the eve descends like a dark-wing'd dove,
O! For a home in that sinless isle,
   In its bowers of bliss to live and love!

John Imlah (1799–1846)

Trembling I sit

FROM *JERUSALEM: THE EMANATION OF THE GIANT ALBION*

Trembling I sit day and night, my friends are astonish'd
   at me.
Yet they forgive my wanderings, I rest not from my great
   task!
To open the Eternal Worlds, to open the immortal Eyes
Of Man inwards into the Worlds of Thought: into
   Eternity
Ever expanding in the Bosom of God, the Human
   Imagination.

William Blake (1757–1827)

Mary's Lamb

Mary had a little lamb,
    Its fleece was white as snow,
And every where that Mary went
    The lamb was sure to go;
He followed her to school one day—
    That was against the rule,
It made the children laugh and play,
    To see a lamb at school.

And so the Teacher turned him out,
    But still he lingered near,
And waited patiently about,
    Till Mary did appear;
And then he ran to her, and laid
    His head upon her arm,
As if he said—'I'm not afraid—
    You'll keep me from all harm.'

'What makes the lamb love Mary so?'
    The eager children cry—
'O, Mary loves the lamb, you know,'
    The Teacher did reply;—
'And you each gentle animal
    In confidence may bind,
And make them follow at your call,
    If you are always *kind*.'

Sarah J. Hale (1788–1879)

Lines

Let us make a leap, my dear,
In our love, of many a year,
And date it very far away,
On a bright clear summer day,
When the heart was like a sun
To itself, and falsehood none;
And the rosy lips a part
Of the very loving heart,
And the shining of the eye
But a sign to know it by;—
When my faults were all forgiven,
And my life deserved of Heaven.
Dearest, let us reckon so,
And love for all that long ago;
Each absence count a year complete,
And keep a birthday when we meet.

Thomas Hood (1799–1845)

MARCH

Little Bird Beside My Window

The World

EXTRACT

I saw Eternity the other night,
Like a great ring of pure and endless light,
All calm, as it was bright;
And round beneath it, Time in hours, days, years,
Driv'n by the spheres
Like a vast shadow mov'd; in which the world
And all her train were hurl'd.

Henry Vaughan (1621–1695)

March

FROM *THE EARTHLY PARADISE*

Slayer of the winter, art thou here again?
O welcome, thou that bring'st the summer nigh!
The bitter wind makes not thy victory vain,
Nor will we mock thee for thy faint blue sky.
Welcome, O March! whose kindly days and dry
Make April ready for the throstle's song,
Thou first redresser of the winter's wrong!

William Morris (1834–1896)

A true and faithful inventory of the goods belonging to doctor Swift, vicar of Laracor; upon his offering to lend his house to the bishop of Meath, until his own was built.

EXTRACT

An oaken, broken, elbow-chair;
A caudle-cup, without an ear;
A batter'd, shatter'd, ash bedstead;
A box of deal, without a lid;
A pair of tongs, but out of joint;
A back-sword poker, without point;
A pot that's cracked across, around,
With an old knotted garter bound;
An iron lock, without a key;
A wig, with hanging quite grown grey;
A curtain, worn to half a stripe;
A pair of bellows, without pipe;
A dish, which might good meat afford once;
An Ovid, and an old Concordance;
A bottle bottom, wooden platter;
One is for meal, and one for water;
There likewise is a copper skillet;
Which runs as fast out, as you fill it;
A candlestick, snuffdish, and save-all,
And thus his household goods you have all.

Thomas Sheridan (1687–1738)

Verses on the Death of Dr. Swift, D.S.P.D.

EXTRACT

   We all behold with envious eyes
Our equal rais'd above our size.
Who would not at a crowded show
Stand high himself, keep others low?
I love my friend as well as you
But would not have him stop my view.
Then let him have the higher post:
I ask but for an inch at most.

   What poet would not grieve to see
His brethren write as well as he?
But rather than they should excel,
He'd wish his rivals all in hell.

   Vain human kind! fantastic race!
Thy various follies who can trace?
Self-love, ambition, envy, pride,
Their empire in our hearts divide.
Give others riches, power, and station,
'Tis all on me a usurpation.
I have no title to aspire;
Yet, when you sink, I seem the higher.

Jonathan Swift (1667–1745)

The Flower

EXTRACT

Who would have thought my shriveled heart
Could have recovered greenness? It was gone
   Quite underground; as flowers depart
To see their mother-root, when they have blown,
    Where they together
    All the hard weather,
  Dead to the world, keep house unknown.

George Herbert (1593–1633)

Those Winter Sundays

Sundays too my father got up early
and put his clothes on in the blueblack cold,
then with cracked hands that ached
from labor in the weekday weather made
banked fires blaze. No one ever thanked him.

I'd wake and hear the cold splintering, breaking.
When the rooms were warm, he'd call,
and slowly I would rise and dress,
fearing the chronic angers of that house,

Speaking indifferently to him,
who had driven out the cold
and polished my good shoes as well.
What did I know, what did I know
of love's austere and lonely offices?

Robert Hayden (1913–1980)

The Housewife

EXTRACT

Food and the serving of food—that is my daylong care;
What and when we shall eat, what and how we shall wear;
Soiling and cleaning of things—that is my task in the
main—
Soil them and clean them and soil them—soil them and
clean them again.

To work at my trade by the dozen and never a trade to
know;
To plan like a Chinese puzzle—fitting and changing so;
To think of a thousand details, each in a thousand ways;
For my own immediate people and a possible love and
praise.

My mind is trodden in circles, tiresome, narrow and hard,
Useful, commonplace, private—simply a small backyard;
And I the Mother of Nations!—Blind their struggle and
vain!—
I cover the earth with my children—each with a
housewife's brain.

Charlotte Anna Perkins Gilman (1860–1935)

Bread and Roses

As we come marching, marching, in the beauty of the day,
A million darkened kitchens, a thousand mill-lofts gray
Are touched with all the radiance that a sudden sun
    discloses,
For the people hear us singing, 'Bread and Roses, Bread
    and Roses.'

As we come marching, marching, we battle, too, for
    men—
For they are women's children and we mother them
again.
Our days shall not be sweated from birth until life
    closes—
Hearts starve as well as bodies: Give us Bread, but give
    us Roses.

As we come marching, marching, unnumbered women
    dead
Go crying through our singing their ancient song of
    Bread;
Small art and love and beauty their trudging spirits
    knew—
Yes, it is Bread we fight for—but we fight for Roses, too.

As we come marching, marching, we bring the Greater
   Days—
The rising of the women means the rising of the race.
No more the drudge and idler—ten that toil where one
   reposes—
But a sharing of life's glories: Bread and Roses, Bread
and Roses.

James Oppenheim (1882–1932)

The Traveller

When March was master of furrow and fold,
And the skies kept cloudy festival
And the daffodil pods were tipped with gold
And a passion was in the plover's call,
A spare old man went hobbling by
With a broken pipe and a tapping stick,
And he mumbled—'Blossom before I die,
Be quick, you little brown buds, be quick.

'I've weathered the world for a count of years—
Good old years of shining fire—
And death and the devil bring no fears,
And I've fed the flame of my last desire;
I'm ready to go, but I'd pass the gate
On the edge of the world with an old heart sick
If I missed the blossoms. I may not wait—
The gate is open—be quick, be quick.'

John Drinkwater (1882–1937)

Leisure

What is this life if, full of care,
We have no time to stand and stare.

No time to stand beneath the boughs
And stare as long as sheep or cows.

No time to see, when woods we pass,
Where squirrels hide their nuts in grass.

No time to see, in broad daylight,
Streams full of stars, like skies at night.

No time to turn at Beauty's glance,
And watch her feet, how they can dance.

No time to wait till her mouth can
Enrich that smile her eyes began.

A poor life this is if, full of care,
We have no time to stand and stare.

W. H. Davies (1871–1940)

To Daffodils

Fair Daffodils, we weep to see
You haste away so soon;
As yet the early-rising sun
Has not attain'd his noon.
Stay, stay,
Until the hasting day
Has run
But to the even-song;
And, having pray'd together, we
Will go with you along.

We have short time to stay, as you,
We have as short a spring;
As quick a growth to meet decay,
As you, or anything.
We die
As your hours do, and dry
Away,
Like to the summer's rain;
Or as the pearls of morning's dew,
Ne'er to be found again.

Robert Herrick (1591–1674)

Spring

Frost-locked all the winter,
Seeds, and roots, and stones of fruits,
What shall make their sap ascend
That they may put forth shoots?
Tips of tender green,
Leaf, or blade, or sheath;
Telling of the hidden life
That breaks forth underneath,
Life nursed in its grave by Death.

Blows the thaw-wind pleasantly,
Drips the soaking rain,
By fits looks down the waking sun:
Young grass springs on the plain;
Young leaves clothe early hedgerow trees;
Seeds, and roots, and stones of fruits,
Swollen with sap put forth their shoots;
Curled-headed ferns sprout in the lane;
Birds sing and pair again.

There is no time like Spring,
When life's alive in everything,
Before new nestlings sing,
Before cleft swallows speed their journey back
Along the trackless track,—
God guides their wing,
He spreads their table that they nothing lack,—
Before the daisy grows a common flower,
Before the sun has power
To scorch the world up in his noontide hour.

There is no time like Spring,
Like Spring that passes by;
There is no life like Spring-life born to die,—
Piercing the sod,
Clothing the uncouth clod,
Hatched in the nest,
Fledged on the windy bough,
Strong on the wing:
There is no time like Spring that passes by,
Now newly born, and now
Hastening to die.

Christina Rossetti (1830–1894)

Between the Showers

Between the showers I went my way,
  The glistening street was bright with flowers;
It seemed that March had turned to May
    Between the showers.

Above the shining roofs and towers
  The blue broke forth athwart the grey;
Birds carolled in their leafless bowers.

Hither and thither, swift and gay,
  The people chased the changeful hours;
And you, you passed and smiled that day,
    Between the showers.

Amy Levy (1861–1889)

There Will Come Soft Rains

(WAR TIME)

There will come soft rains and the smell of the ground,
And swallows circling with their shimmering sound;

And frogs in the pools singing at night,
And wild plum trees in tremulous white;

Robins will wear their feathery fire
Whistling their whims on a low fence-wire;

And not one will know of the war, not one
Will care at last when it is done.

Not one would mind, neither bird nor tree
If mankind perished utterly;

And Spring herself, when she woke at dawn,
Would scarcely know that we were gone.

Sara Teasdale (1884–1933)

I wandered lonely as a cloud

I wandered lonely as a cloud
That floats on high o'er vales and hills,
When all at once I saw a crowd,
A host, of golden daffodils;
Beside the lake, beneath the trees,
Fluttering and dancing in the breeze.

Continuous as the stars that shine
And twinkle on the milky way,
They stretched in never-ending line
Along the margin of a bay:
Ten thousand saw I at a glance,
Tossing their heads in sprightly dance.

The waves beside them danced; but they
Out-did the sparkling waves in glee;
A poet could not but be gay,
In such a jocund company:
I gazed—and gazed—but little thought
What wealth the show to me had brought:

For oft, when on my couch I lie
In vacant or in pensive mood,
They flash upon that inward eye
Which is the bliss of solitude;
And then my heart with pleasure fills,
And dances with the daffodils.

William Wordsworth (1770–1850)

The Sparrow

A little bird, with plumage brown,
Beside my window flutters down,
A moment chirps its little strain,
Ten taps upon my window-pane,
And chirps again, and hops along,
To call my notice to its song;
But I work on, nor heed its lay,
Till, in neglect, it flies away.

So birds of peace and hope and love
Come fluttering earthward from above,
To settle on life's window-sills,
And ease our load of earthly ills;
But we, in traffic's rush and din
Too deep engaged to let them in,
With deadened heart and sense plod on,
Nor know our loss till they are gone.

Paul Laurence Dunbar (1872–1906)

May the road rise up to meet you

TRADITIONAL GAELIC BLESSING

May the road rise up to meet you.
May the wind be always at your back.
May the sun shine warm upon your face;
the rains fall soft upon your fields
and until we meet again,
may God hold you in the palm of His hand.

Anon

Pittypat and Tippytoe

EXTRACT

All day long they come and go—
Pittypat and Tippytoe;
Footprints up and down the hall,
  Playthings scattered on the floor,
Finger-marks along the wall,
  Tell-tale streaks upon the door—
By these presents you shall know
Pittypat and Tippytoe.

How they riot at their play!
And, a dozen times a day
  In they troop, demanding bread—
    Only buttered bread will do,
  And that butter must be spread
    Inches thick with sugar too!
Never yet have I said, 'No,
Pittypat and Tippytoe!'

On the floor along the hall,
Rudely traced upon the wall,
  There are proofs in every kind
    Of the havoc they have wrought,
  And upon my heart you'd find
    Just such trademarks, if you sought.
Oh, how glad I am 'tis so,
Pittypat and Tippytoe!

Eugene Field (1850–1895)

Have you got a brook in your little heart

Have you got a brook in your little heart,
Where bashful flowers blow,
And blushing birds go down to drink,
And shadows tremble so?

And nobody knows, so still it flows,
That any brook is there;
And yet your little draught of life
Is daily drunken there.

Then look out for the little brook in March,
When the rivers overflow,
And the snows come hurrying from the hills,
And the bridges often go.

And later, in August it may be,
When the meadows parching lie,
Beware, lest this little brook of life,
Some burning noon go dry!

Emily Dickinson (1830–1886)

Spring Flowers

FROM *SPRING, A POEM*

Along the blushing Borders, dewy-bright,
And in yon mingled Wilderness of Flowers,
Fair-handed *Spring* unbosoms every Grace;
Throws out the Snow-Drop, and the Crocus first,
The Daisy, Primrose, Violet darkly blue,
Soft-bending Cowslips, and of nameless Dies
Anemonies, Auriculas, a Tribe
Peculiar powder'd with a shining Sand,
Renunculas, and Iris many-hued.
Then comes the Tulip-Race, where Beauty plays
Her gayest Freaks; from Family diffus'd
To Family, as flies the Father-Dust,
The varied Colours run; and while they break
On the charm'd *Florist's* Eye, he wondering stands,
And new-flush'd Glories all ecstatic marks.
        * * * *

Infinite Numbers, Delicacies, Smells,
With Hues on Hues Expression cannot paint,
The Breath of *Nature,* and her endless Bloom.

James Thomson (1700–1748)

I could never have dreamt

FROM THE ESSAY *NOTES ON THE ART OF POETRY*

I could never have dreamt that there were such goings-on
in the world between the covers of books,
such sandstorms and ice blasts of words,
such staggering peace, such enormous laughter,
such and so many blinding bright lights
splashing all over the pages
in a million bits and pieces
all of which were words, words, words,
and each of which were alive forever
in its own delight and glory and oddity and light.

Dylan Thomas (1914–1953)

It is a fearful stake the poet casts

FROM THE NOVEL *ETHEL CHURCHILL*

It is a fearful stake the poet casts,
When he comes forth from his sweet solitude
Of hopes, and songs, and visionary things,
To ask the iron verdict of the world.
Till then his home has been in fairyland,
Sheltered in the sweet depths of his own heart;
But the strong need of praise impels him forth;
For never was there poet but he craved
The golden sunshine of secure renown.
That sympathy which is the life of fame,
It is full dearly bought: henceforth he lives
Feverish and anxious, in an unkind world.
That only gives the laurel to the grave.

L. E. L. (Elizabeth Letitia Landon) (1802–1838)

She dwelt among the untrodden ways

She dwelt among the untrodden ways
Beside the springs of Dove,
A Maid whom there were none to praise
And very few to love:

A violet by a mossy stone
Half hidden from the eye!
—Fair as a star, when only one
Is shining in the sky.

She lived unknown, and few could know
When Lucy ceased to be;
But she is in her grave, and, oh,
The difference to me!

William Wordsworth (1770–1850)

London Bells

Two Sticks and Apple,
Ring ye Bells at Whitechapple,

Old Father Bald Pate,
Ring ye Bells Aldgate,

Maids in White Aprons,
Ring ye Bells at St. Catherines,

Oranges and Lemons,
Ring ye bells at St. Clements,

When will you pay me,
Ring ye Bells at ye Old Bailey,

When I am Rich,
Ring ye Bells at Fleetditch,

When will that be,
Ring ye Bells at Stepney,

When I am Old,
Ring ye Bells at Pauls.

Anon

Sudden Shower

Black grows the southern sky betokening rain
And humming hive-bees homeward hurry by
They feel the change—so let us shun the grain
And take the broad road while our feet are dry.
Ay, there some dropples moistened in my face
And pattered on my hat—'tis coming nigh—
Let's look about, and find a sheltering place.
The little things around, like you and I,
Are hurrying through the grass to shun the shower.
Here stoops an ash tree—hark, the wind gets high,
But never mind; this ivy, for an hour,
Rain as it may, will keep us dryly here.
That little wren knows well his sheltering bower,
Nor leaves his dry house though we come so near.

John Clare (1793–1864)

A Nocturnal Reverie

EXTRACT

But silent musings urge the mind to seek
Something, too high for syllables to speak;
Till the free soul to a composedness charmed,
Finding the elements of rage disarmed,
O'er all below a solemn quiet grown,
Joys in th' inferior world, and thinks it like her own:
In such a night let me abroad remain,
Till morning breaks, and all's confused again;
Our cares, our toils, our clamors are renewed,
Or pleasures, seldom reached, again pursued.

Anne Finch, Countess of Winchilsea (1661–1720)

When to the sessions of sweet silent thought

SONNET XXX

When to the sessions of sweet silent thought
I summon up remembrance of things past,
I sigh the lack of many a thing I sought,
And with old woes new wail my dear time's waste:
Then can I drown an eye, unused to flow,
For precious friends hid in death's dateless night,
And weep afresh love's long since cancelled woe,
And moan th' expense of many a vanished sight;
Then can I grieve at grievances foregone,
And heavily from woe to woe tell o'er
The sad account of fore-bemoanèd moan,
Which I new pay as if not paid before.
    But if the while I think on thee, dear friend,
    All losses are restored, and sorrows end.

William Shakespeare (1564–1616)

The God Abandons Antony

When suddenly, at midnight, you hear
an invisible procession going by
with exquisite music, voices,
don't mourn your luck that's failing now,
work gone wrong, your plans
all proving deceptive—don't mourn them uselessly.
As one long prepared, and graced with courage,
say goodbye to her, the Alexandria that is leaving.
Above all, don't fool yourself, don't say
it was a dream, your ears deceived you:
don't degrade yourself with empty hopes like these.
As one long prepared, and graced with courage,
as is right for you who proved worthy of this kind of city,
go firmly to the window
and listen with deep emotion, but not
with the whining, the pleas of a coward;
listen—your final delectation—to the voices,
to the exquisite music of that strange procession,
and say goodbye to her, to the Alexandria you are losing.

C. P. Cavafy (1863–1933)
Translated from the Greek by Edmund Keeley (1928–2022) and
Philip Sherrard (1922–1995)

All nature has a feeling

All nature has a feeling wood brooks fields
Are life eternal—and in silence they
Speak happiness—beyond the reach of books
There's nothing mortal in them—their decay
Is the green life of change; to pass away
And come again in blooms revified
Its birth was heaven eternal is its stay
And with the sun and moon shall still abide
Beneath their night and day and heaven wide

John Clare (1793–1864)

The saddest noise, the sweetest noise

The saddest noise, the sweetest noise,
The maddest noise that grows,—
The birds, they make it in the spring,
At night's delicious close,

Between the March and April line—
That magical frontier
Beyond which summer hesitates,
Almost too heavenly near.

It makes us think of all the dead
That sauntered with us here,
By separation's sorcery
Made cruelly more dear.

It makes us think of what we had,
And what we now deplore.
We almost wish those siren throats
Would go and sing no more.

An ear can break a human heart
As quickly as a spear,
We wish the ear had not a heart
So dangerously near.

Emily Dickinson (1830–1886)

All That's Past

Very old are the woods;
  And the buds that break
Out of the brier's boughs,
  When March winds wake,
So old with their beauty are—
  Oh, no man knows
Through what wild centuries
Roves back the rose.

Very old are the brooks;
  And the rills that rise
Where snow sleeps cold beneath
  The azure skies
Sing such a history
  Of come and gone,
Their every drop is as wise
  As Solomon.

Very old are we men;
  Our dreams are tales
Told in dim Eden
  By Eve's nightingales;
We wake and whisper awhile,
  But, the day gone by,
Silence and sleep like fields
  Of amaranth lie.

Walter de la Mare (1873–1956)

APRIL

Hear the Seed Sprout

The Baker's Tale

FROM *THE HUNTING OF THE SNARK*

They roused him with muffins—they roused him with ice—
  They roused him with mustard and cress—
They roused him with jam and judicious advice—
  They set him conundrums to guess.

When at length he sat up and was able to speak,
  His sad story he offered to tell;
And the Bellman cried 'Silence! Not even a shriek!'
  And excitedly tingled his bell.

There was silence supreme! Not a shriek, not a scream,
  Scarcely even a howl or a groan,
As the man they called 'Ho!' told his story of woe
  In an antediluvian tone.

'My father and mother were honest, though poor—'
  'Skip all that!' cried the Bellman in haste.
'If it once becomes dark, there's no chance of a Snark—
  We have hardly a minute to waste!'

'I skip forty years,' said the Baker, in tears,
  'And proceed without further remark
To the day when you took me aboard of your ship
  To help you in hunting the Snark.

'A dear uncle of mine (after whom I was named)
    Remarked, when I bade him farewell—'
'Oh, skip your dear uncle!' the Bellman exclaimed,
    As he angrily tingled his bell.

'He remarked to me then,' said that mildest of men,
    '"If your Snark be a Snark, that is right:
Fetch it home by all means—you may serve it with
    greens,
    And it's handy for striking a light.

'"You may seek it with thimbles—and seek it with care;
    You may hunt it with forks and hope;
You may threaten its life with a railway-share;
    You may charm it with smiles and soap—"'

('That's exactly the method,' the Bellman bold
    In a hasty parenthesis cried,
'That's exactly the way I have always been told
    That the capture of Snarks should be tried!')

'"But oh, beamish nephew, beware of the day,
    If your Snark be a Boojum! For then
You will softly and suddenly vanish away,
    And never be met with again!"

'It is this, it is this that oppresses my soul,
   When I think of my uncle's last words:
And my heart is like nothing so much as a bowl
   Brimming over with quivering curds!

'It is this, it is this—' 'We have had that before!'
   The Bellman indignantly said.
And the Baker replied 'Let me say it once more.
   It is this, it is this that I dread!

'I engage with the Snark—every night after dark—
   In a dreamy delirious fight:
I serve it with greens in those shadowy scenes,
   And I use it for striking a light;

'But if ever I meet with a Boojum, that day,
   In a moment (of this I am sure),
I shall softly and suddenly vanish away—
   And the notion I cannot endure!'

Lewis Carroll (1832–1898)

The Cryes of London

Hark! how the Cries in every street make lanes and allies
ring:
With their goods and ware both nice and rare,
All in a pleasant lofty strain;
Come buy my gudgeons fine and new.
Old cloaths to change for earthen ware.
Come taste and try before you buy, here's dainty poplin
pears.
Diddle, diddle, diddle dumplins, ho! with walnuts nice
and brown.
Let none despise the merry, merry cries of famous London
town.

Here's fine rosemary, sage, and thyme. Come buy my
ground-ivy.
Here's fetherfew, gilliflowers and rue.
Come buy my knotted marjorum, ho!
Come buy my mint, my fine green mint. Here's fine
lavender for your cloaths.
Here's parsley, and winter-savory. And heart's ease,
which all do choose.
Here's balm and hissop, and cinquefoil, all fine herbs, it
is well known.
Let none despise the merry, merry cries of famous London
town.

Here's pennyroyal and marygolds. Come buy my
   nettle-tops.
Here's water-cresses and scurvy-grass.
   Come buy my sage, of virtue, ho!
Come buy my wormwood and mug-wort. Here's all fine
herbs of every sort.
Here's southernwood that's very good, dandelion and
houseleek.
Here's dragon's-tongue and wood-sorrel, with bear's-foot
and horehound.
*Let none despise the merry, merry cries of famous London
   town.*

Anon

Fairy folk a-listening

EPIGRAM FROM THE NOVEL *DANIEL DERONDA*

Fairy folk a-listening
Hear the seed sprout in the spring.
And for music to their dance
Hear the hedgerows wake from trance,
Sap that trembles into buds
Sending little rhythmic floods
Of fairy sound in fairy ears.
Thus all beauty that appears
Has birth as sound to finer sense
And lighter-clad intelligence.

George Eliot (1819–1880)

From a Railway Carriage

Faster than fairies, faster than witches,
Bridges and houses, hedges and ditches;
And charging along like troops in a battle,
All through the meadows the horses and cattle:
All of the sights of the hill and the plain
Fly as thick as driving rain;
And ever again, in the wink of an eye,
Painted stations whistle by.

Here is a child who clambers and scrambles,
All by himself and gathering brambles;
Here is a tramp who stands and gazes;
And there is the green for stringing the daisies!
Here is a cart run away in the road
Lumping along with man and load;
And here is a mill and there is a river:
Each a glimpse and gone for ever!

Robert Louis Stevenson (1850–1894)

Appeal

Daphnis dearest, wherefore weave me
Webs of lies lest truth should grieve me?
I could pardon much, believe me:
Dower me, Daphnis, or bereave me,
Kiss me, kill me, love me, leave me,—
Damn me, dear, but don't deceive me!

E. Nesbit (1858–1924)

I am both Glass and Image

FROM *THE SOUL IN ALL*

I am both Glass and Image; the Echo and the Call.
I am the Tree and Branches, and all the Birds thereon;
I am both Thought and Silence, Tongues' Speech, and
  Ocean Squall.
I am the Flute when piping, and Man's Soul breathing
  breath.

Rumi (1207–1273)
Translated from the Persian by William Hastie (1842–1903)

Now fades the last long streak of snow

FROM *IN MEMORIAM A.H.H.*

Now fades the last long streak of snow,
  Now burgeons every maze of quick
  About the flowering squares, and thick
By ashen roots the violets blow.

Now rings the woodland loud and long,
  The distance takes a lovelier hue,
  And drown'd in yonder living blue
The lark becomes a sightless song.

Now dance the lights on lawn and lea,
  The flocks are whiter down the vale,
  And milkier every milky sail
On winding stream or distant sea;

Where now the sea-mew pipes, or dives
  In yonder greening gleam, and fly
  The happy birds, that change their sky
To build and brood; that live their lives

From land to land; and in my breast
  Spring wakens too; and my regret
  Becomes an April violet,
And buds and blossoms like the rest.

Alfred, Lord Tennyson (1809–1892)

Spring

Nothing is so beautiful as Spring—
When weeds, in wheels, shoot long and lovely and lush;
   Thrush's eggs look little low heavens, and thrush
Through the echoing timber does so rinse and wring
The ear, it strikes like lightnings to hear him sing;
   The glassy peartree leaves and blooms, they brush
   The descending blue; that blue is all in a rush
With richness; the racing lambs too have fair their fling.

What is all this juice and all this joy?
   A strain of the earth's sweet being in the beginning
In Eden garden.—Have, get, before it cloy,

   Before it cloud, Christ, lord, and sour with sinning,
Innocent mind and Mayday in girl and boy,
   Most, O maid's child, thy choice and worthy the
   winning.

Gerard Manley Hopkins (1844–1889)

To Any Reader

As from the house your mother sees
You playing round the garden trees,
So you may see, if you will look
Through the windows of this book,
Another child, far, far away,
And in another garden, play.
But do not think you can at all,
By knocking on the window, call
That child to hear you. He intent
Is all on his play-business bent.
He does not hear; he will not look,
Nor yet be lured out of this book.
For, long ago, the truth to say,
He has grown up and gone away,
And it is but a child of air
That lingers in the garden there.

Robert Louis Stevenson (1850–1894)

Home Thoughts From Abroad

Oh, to be in England
Now that April's there,
And whoever wakes in England
Sees, some morning, unaware,
That the lowest boughs and the brushwood sheaf
Round the elm-tree bole are in tiny leaf,
While the chaffinch sings on the orchard bough
In England—now!

And after April, when May follows,
And the white-throat builds, and all the swallows!
Hark, where my blossomed pear tree in the hedge
Leans to the field and scatters on the clover
Blossoms and dewdrops—at the bent spray's edge—
That's the wise thrush: he sings each song twice over,
Lest you should think he never could recapture
The first fine careless rapture!
And, though the fields look rough with hoary dew,
All will be gay when noontide wakes anew
The buttercups, the little children's dower,
—Far brighter than this gaudy melon-flower!

Robert Browning (1812–1889)

Loveliest of trees, the cherry now

FROM *A SHROPSHIRE LAD*

Loveliest of trees, the cherry now
Is hung with bloom along the bough,
And stands about the woodland ride
Wearing white for Eastertide.

Now, of my threescore years and ten,
Twenty will not come again,
And take from seventy springs a score,
It only leaves me fifty more.

And since to look at things in bloom
Fifty springs are little room,
About the woodlands I will go
To see the cherry hung with snow.

A. E. Housman (1859–1936)

'Tis a strange mystery, the power of words

FROM THE NOVEL *ETHEL CHURCHILL*

'Tis a strange mystery, the power of words!
Life is in them, and death. A word can send
The crimson colour hurrying to the cheek.
Hurrying with many meanings; or can turn
The current cold and deadly to the heart.
Anger and fear are in them; grief and joy
Are on their sound; yet slight, impalpable:—
A word is but a breath of passing air.

L. E. L. (Elizabeth Letitia Landon) (1802–1838)

Renouncement

I must not think of thee; and, tired yet strong,
I shun the love that lurks in all delight—
The love of thee—and in the blue heaven's height,
And in the dearest passage of a song.
Oh, just beyond the sweetest thoughts that throng
This breast, the thought of thee waits hidden yet bright;
But it must never, never come in sight;
I must stop short of thee the whole day long.
But when sleep comes to close each difficult day,
When night gives pause to the long watch I keep,
And all my bonds I needs must loose apart,
Must doff my will as raiment laid away,—
With the first dream that comes with the first sleep
I run, I run, I am gather'd to thy heart.

Alice Meynell (1847–1922)

Weathers

This is the weather the cuckoo likes,
   And so do I;
When showers betumble the chestnut spikes,
   And nestlings fly;
And the little brown nightingale bills his best,
And they sit outside at 'The Travellers' Rest,'
And maids come forth sprig-muslin drest,
And citizens dream of the south and west,
   And so do I.

This is the weather the shepherd shuns,
   And so do I;
When beeches drip in browns and duns,
   And thresh, and ply;
And hill-hid tides throb, throe on throe,
And meadow rivulets overflow,
And drops on gate-bars hang in a row,
And rooks in families homeward go,
   And so do I.

Thomas Hardy (1840–1928)

Walking

EXTRACT

To walk is by a thought to go;
To move in spirit to and fro;
To mind the good we see;
To taste the sweet;
Observing all the things we meet
How choice and rich they be.

To note the beauty of the day,
And golden fields of corn survey;
Admire each pretty flow'r
With its sweet smell;
To praise their Maker, and to tell
The marks of his great pow'r.
* * * *
Observe those rich and glorious things,
The rivers, meadows, woods, and springs,
The fructifying sun;
To note from far
The rising of each twinkling star
For us his race to run.

A little child these well perceives,
Who, tumbling in green grass and leaves,
May rich as kings be thought,
But there's a sight
Which perfect manhood may delight,
To which we shall be brought.

While in those pleasant paths we talk,
'Tis that tow'rds which at last we walk;
For we may by degrees
Wisely proceed
Pleasures of love and praise to heed,
From viewing herbs and trees.

Thomas Traherne (c. 1636–1674)

On a Lane in Spring

A little lane, the brook runs close beside
  And spangles in the sunshine while the fish glide
  swiftly by,
And hedges leafing with the green spring tide:
  From out their greenery the old birds fly,
And chirp and whistle in the morning sun:
  The pilewort glitters 'neath the pale blue sky,
The little robin has its nest begun
  And grass green linnets round the bushes fly.
How Mild the Spring Comes in! The daisy buds
  Lift up their golden blossoms to the sky
How lovely are the pingles and the woods!
  Here a beetle runs, and there a fly
Rests on the arum leaf in bottle green,
  And all the spring in this green lane is seen.

John Clare (1793–1864)

The Ballad of Henry and Nancy; or the Lover's Separation

As I walked out one morning in the springtime of the
year,
I overheard a sailor bold, likewise a lady fair:
They sung a song together that made the vallies ring,
Whilst the birds on sprays and meadows gay proclaim'd a
   lovely spring.

Said Henry to Nancy I must soon sail away,
It is lovely on the water to hear the music play.
The Queen she does want seamen so I'll not stay on
shore,
So I'll brave the wars for my country's cause cannons
   loudly roar.

Oh, then said pretty Nancy pray stay at home with me,
Or let me go along with you to bear your company,
I'll put on a pair of trousers and leave my native shore,
Then let me go along with you where cannons
   loud do roar.

It will not do said Henry, it's in vain for you to try.
They will not ship a female, young Henry did reply;
Besides your hands are delicate, the ropes would make
   them sore,
T'would be worse if you should fall where the cannon
   loudly roar.

Four pounds is the bounty, and that would do for thee,
To help thy aged parents while I am far at sea.
Come, change your ring with me, my love, for we may
    meet once more,
For one above may guard your love where cannons
    loudly roar.

Poor Nancy fell and fainted but soon they brought her to,
They then shook hands together and took a fond adieu.
The Tower-hill was crowded with mothers weeping sore,
For sons that's gone to face the foe where cannons
    loudly roar.

There's many a mother's darling has entered for the main,
And in the dreadful battles what numbers will be slain;
For many a weeping mother and widow will deplore,
For those who fall by cannon balls where cannons
    loudly roar.

Anon

Say Over Again

Say over again, and yet once over again,
That thou dost love me. Though the word repeated
Should seem 'a cuckoo-song,' as thou dost treat it,
Remember, never to the hill or plain,
Valley and wood, without her cuckoo-strain
Comes the fresh Spring in all her green completed.
Belovèd, I, amid the darkness greeted
By a doubtful spirit-voice, in that doubt's pain
Cry, 'Speak once more—thou lovest!' Who can fear
Too many stars, though each in heaven shall roll,
Too many flowers, though each shall crown the year?
Say thou dost love me, love me, love me—toll
The silver iterance!—only minding, Dear,
To love me also in silence with thy soul.

Elizabeth Barrett Browning (1806–1861)

Repeat that, repeat

Repeat that, repeat,
Cuckoo, bird, and open ear wells, heart-springs,
    delightfully sweet,
With a ballad, with a ballad, a rebound
Off trundled timber and scoops of the hillside ground,
    hollow hollow hollow ground:
The whole landscape flushes on a sudden at a sound.

Gerard Manley Hopkins (1844–1889)

The Butter Betty Bought

Betty Botta bought some butter;
'But,' said she, 'this butter's bitter!
If I put it in my batter
It will make my batter bitter.
But a bit o' better butter
Will but make my batter better.'
Then she bought a bit o' butter
Better than the bitter butter,
Made her bitter batter better.
So 'twas better Betty Botta
Bought a bit o' better butter.

Carolyn Wells (1862–1942)

A word

A word is dead, when it is said,
Some say—
I say it just begins to live
That day

Emily Dickinson (1830–1886)

Inversnaid

EXTRACT

What would the world be, once bereft
Of wet and of wildness? Let them be left,
O let them be left, wildness and wet;
Long live the weeds and the wilderness yet.

Gerard Manley Hopkins (1844–1889)

And did those feet

FROM *MILTON*

And did those feet in ancient time
Walk upon England's mountains green?
And was the holy Lamb of God
On England's pleasant pastures seen?

And did the Countenance Divine,
Shine forth upon our clouded hills?
And was Jerusalem builded here,
Among these dark Satanic Mills?

Bring me my Bow of burning gold:
Bring me my arrows of desire:
Bring me my Spear: O clouds unfold:
Bring me my Chariot of fire!

I will not cease from Mental Fight,
Nor shall my sword sleep in my hand,
Till we have built Jerusalem
In England's green & pleasant Land.

William Blake (1757–1827)

Reciprocity

I do not think that skies and meadows are
Moral, or that the fixture of a star
Comes of a quiet spirit, or that trees
Have wisdom in their windless silences.
Yet these are things invested in my mood
With constancy, and peace, and fortitude,
That in my troubled season I can cry
Upon the wide composure of the sky,
And envy fields, and wish that I might be
As little daunted as a star or tree.

John Drinkwater (1882–1937)

Song of the River

FROM *THE WATER BABIES*

Clear and cool, clear and cool,
By laughing shallow and dreaming pool;
Cool and clear, cool and clear,
By shining shingle and foaming weir;
Under the crag where the ouzel sings,
And the ivied wall where the church-bell rings,
Undefiled for the undefiled;
Play by me, bathe in me, mother and child!

Dank and foul, dank and foul,
By the smoky town in its murky cowl;
Foul and dank, foul and dank,
By wharf, and sewer, and slimy bank;
Darker and darker the further I go.
Baser and baser the richer I grow;
Who dare sport with the sin-defiled?
Shrink from me, turn from me, mother and child!

Strong and free, strong and free,
The flood-gates are open, away to the sea:
Free and strong, free and strong,
Cleansing my streams as I hurry along
To the golden sands and the leaping bar,
And the taintless tide that awaits me afar,
As I lose myself in the infinite main,
Like a soul that has sinned and is pardoned again,
Undefiled for the undefiled;
Play by me, bathe in me, mother and child!

Charles Kingsley (1819–1875)

Is it so small a thing

FROM *THE HYMN OF EMPEDOCLES*

Is it so small a thing
To have enjoy'd the sun,
To have lived light in the spring,
To have loved, to have thought, to have done;
To have advanced true friends, and beat down baffling
  foes;

That we must feign a bliss
Of doubtful future date,
  And while we dream on this
Lose all our present state,
And relegate to worlds yet distant our repose?
        * * * *

I say, Fear not! life still
Leaves human effort scope.
But, since life teems with ill,
Nurse no extravagant hope.
Because thou must not dream, thou need'st not then
  despair.

Matthew Arnold (1822–1888)

O for a booke

O for a booke and a shadie nooke,
  eyther indoore or out;
With the grene leaves whispering overheade,
  or the streete cryes all about.
Where I maie reade all at my ease,
  both of the newe and olde;
For a jollie goode Booke whereon to looke,
  is better to me than golde.

Anon

The Argument of His Book

I sing of brooks, of blossoms, birds, and bowers,
Of April, May, of June, and July-flowers.
I sing of Maypoles, hock-carts, wassails, wakes,
Of bridegrooms, brides, and of their bridal cakes.
I write of youth, of love, and have access
By these to sing of cleanly wantonness.
I sing of dews, of rains, and, piece by piece,
Of balm, of oil, of spice, and ambergris.
I sing of time's trans-shifting; and I write
How roses first came red, and lilies white.
I write of groves, of twilights, and I sing
The court of Mab, and of the Fairy King.
I write of Hell; I sing (and ever shall)
Of Heaven, and hope to have it after all.

Robert Herrick (1591–1674)

My heart leaps up

My heart leaps up when I behold
   A Rainbow in the sky:
So was it when my life began;
So is it now I am a Man:
So be it when I shall grow old,
   Or let me die!
The Child is Father of the Man;
And I could wish my days to be
Bound each to each by natural piety.

William Wordsworth (1770–1850)

All the Pretty Little Horses

LULLABY

Hush you bye, Don't you cry,
Go to sleepy, little baby.
When you wake,
You shall have,
all the pretty little horses.
Blacks and Bays,
dapples and grays,
Coach and six a little horses.
Hush-a-by, Don't you cry,
Go to sleep, my little baby.

Anon

MAY

Dearest Freshness Deep Down

The Passionate Shepherd to His Love

Come live with me and be my love,
And we will all the pleasures prove
That valleys, groves, hills, and fields,
Woods, or steepy mountain yields.

And we will sit upon the rocks,
Seeing the shepherds feed their flocks,
By shallow rivers to whose falls
Melodious birds sing madrigals.

And I will make thee beds of roses
And a thousand fragrant posies,
A cap of flowers, and a kirtle
Embroidered all with leaves of myrtle;

A gown made of the finest wool
Which from our pretty lambs we pull;
Fair lined slippers for the cold,
With buckles of the purest gold;

A belt of straw and ivy buds,
With coral clasps and amber studs:
And if these pleasures may thee move,
Come live with me and be my love.

The shepherds' swains shall dance and sing
For thy delight each May morning:
If these delights thy mind may move,
Then live with me and be my love

Christopher Marlowe (1564–1593)

The Nymph's Reply to the Shepherd

If all the world and love were young,
And truth in every shepherd's tongue,
These pretty pleasures might me move
To live with thee and be thy love.

Time drives the flocks from field to fold
When rivers rage and rocks grow cold,
And Philomel becometh dumb;
The rest complains of cares to come.

The flowers do fade, and wanton fields
To wayward winter reckoning yields:
A honey tongue, a heart of gall,
Is fancy's spring, but sorrow's fall.

Thy gowns, thy shoes, thy beds of roses,
Thy cap, thy kirtle, and thy posies
Soon break, soon wither, soon forgotten,—
In folly ripe, in reason rotten.

Thy belt of straw and Ivy buds,
Thy coral clasps and amber studs,—
All these in me no means can move
To come to thee and be thy love.

But could youth last and love still breed;
Had joys no date nor age no need;
Then these delights my mind might move
To live with thee and be thy love.

Sir Walter Ralegh (1554–1618)

Dawn Talks to Day

FROM *SONG VII*

Dawn talks to Day
Over dew-gleaming flowers,
Night flies away
Till the resting of hours:
Fresh are thy feet
And with dreams thine eyes glistening,
Thy still lips are sweet
Though the world is a-listening.
O Love, set a word in my mouth for our meeting,
Cast thine arms round about me to stay my heart's
    beating!
O fresh day, O fair day, O long day made ours!

William Morris (1834–1896)

The Peace of Wild Things

When despair for the world grows in me
and I wake in the night at the least sound
in fear of what my life and my children's lives may be,
I go and lie down where the wood drake
rests in his beauty on the water, and the great heron feeds.
I come into the peace of wild things
who do not tax their lives with forethought
of grief. I come into the presence of still water.
And I feel above me the day-blind stars
waiting with their light. For a time
I rest in the grace of the world, and am free.

Wendell Berry (b.1934)

Answer to a Child's Question

Do you ask what the birds say? The Sparrow, the Dove,
The Linnet and Thrush say, 'I love and I love!'
In the winter they're silent—the wind is so strong;
What it says, I don't know, but it sings a loud song.
But green leaves, and blossoms, and sunny warm
    weather,
And singing, and loving—all come back together.
But the Lark is so brimful of gladness and love,
The green fields below him, the blue sky above,
That he sings, and he sings; and for ever sings he—
'I love my Love, and my Love loves me!'

Samuel Taylor Coleridge (1772–1834)

The Changeling

EXTRACT

Sometimes I wouldn't speak, you see,
  Or answer when you spoke to me,
Because in the long, still dusks of Spring
You can hear the whole world whispering;
  The shy green grasses making love,
  The feathers grow on the dear, grey dove,
  The tiny heart of the redstart beat,
  The patter of the squirrel's feet,
The pebbles pushing in the silver streams,
The rushes talking in their dreams,
  The swish-swish of the bat's black wings,
  The wild-wood bluebell's sweet ting-tings,
    Humming and hammering at your ear,
    Everything there is to hear
In the heart of hidden things ...

Charlotte Mew (1869–1928)

Hours

I have known hours built like cities,
House on grey house, with streets between
That lead to straggling roads and trail off,
Forgotten in a field of green;

Hours made like mountains lifting
White crests out of the fog and rain,
And woven of forbidden music—
Hours eternal in their pain.

Life is a tapestry of hours
Forever mellowing in tone,
Where all things blend, even the longing
For hours I have never known

Hazel Hall (1886–1924)

God's Grandeur

The world is charged with the grandeur of God.
   It will flame out, like shining from shook foil;
   It gathers to a greatness, like the ooze of oil
Crushed. Why do men then now not reck his rod?
Generations have trod, have trod, have trod;
   And all is seared with trade; bleared, smeared with toil;
   And wears man's smudge and shares man's smell: the soil
Is bare now, nor can foot feel, being shod.

And for all this, nature is never spent;
   There lives the dearest freshness deep down things;
And though the last lights off the black West went
   Oh, morning, at the brown brink eastward, springs—
Because the Holy Ghost over the bent
   World broods with warm breast and with ah! bright
   wings.

Gerard Manley Hopkins (1844–1889)

Heraclitus

They told me, Heraclitus, they told me you were dead,
They brought me bitter news to hear and bitter tears to
   shed,
I wept, as I remembered, how often you and I
Had tired the sun with talking, and sent him down the sky.

And now that thou art lying, my dear old Carian guest,
A handful of grey ashes, long, long ago at rest,
Still are thy pleasant voices, thy nightingales, awake;
For Death, he taketh all away, but them he cannot take.

Callimachus (c. 310/305–c. 240 BC)
Translated from the Greek by William Johnson Cory (1823–1892)

My own voice

FROM *THE PRELUDE* (1805), BOOK I

My own voice cheared me, and, far more, the mind's
Internal echo of the imperfect sound;
To both I listened, drawing from them both
A cheerful confidence in things to come.

William Wordsworth (1770–1850)

This royal throne of kings

FROM *RICHARD II*, ACT II, SCENE I

This royal throne of kings, this sceptered isle,
This earth of majesty, this seat of Mars,
This other Eden, demi-paradise,
This fortress built by Nature for herself
Against infection and the hand of war,
This happy breed of men, this little world,
This precious stone set in the silver sea,
Which serves it in the office of a wall,
Or as a moat defensive to a house,
Against the envy of less happier lands,
This blessed plot, this earth, this realm, this England,
This nurse, this teeming womb of royal kings,
     * * * *

This land of such dear souls, this dear dear land,
Dear for her reputation through the world,
Is now leased out—I die pronouncing it—
Like to a tenement or pelting farm:
England, bound in with the triumphant sea
Whose rocky shore beats back the envious siege
Of watery Neptune, is now bound in with shame,
With inky blots and rotten parchment bonds:
That England, that was wont to conquer others,
Hath made a shameful conquest of itself.
Ah, would the scandal vanish with my life,
How happy then were my ensuing death!

William Shakespeare (1564–1616)

The Child in the Garden

When to the garden of untroubled thought
  I came of late, and saw the open door,
  And wished again to enter, and explore
The sweet, wild ways with stainless bloom inwrought,
And bowers of innocence with beauty fraught,
  It seemed some purer voice must speak before
  I dared to tread that garden loved of yore,
That Eden lost unknown and found unsought.

Then just within the gate I saw a child,—
  A stranger-child, yet to my heart most dear;
He held his hands to me, and softly smiled
  With eyes that knew no shade of sin or fear:
'Come in,' he said, 'and play awhile with me;'
'I am the little child you used to be.'

Henry Van Dyke (1852–1933)

For These

An acre of land between the shore and the hills,
Upon a ledge that shows my kingdoms three,
The lovely visible earth and sky and sea,
Where what the curlew needs not, the farmer tills:

A house that shall love me as I love it,
Well-hedged, and honoured by a few ash trees
That linnets, greenfinches, and goldfinches
Shall often visit and make love in and flit:

A garden I need never go beyond,
Broken but neat, whose sunflowers every one
Are fit to be the sign of the Rising Sun:
A spring, a brook's bend, or at least a pond:

For these I ask not, but, neither too late
Nor yet too early, for what men call content,
And also that something may be sent
To be contented with, I ask of Fate.

Edward Thomas (1878–1917)

I So Liked Spring

I so liked Spring last year
  Because you were here;—
    The thrushes too—
Because it was these you so liked to hear—
    I so liked you.

  This year's a different thing,—
    I'll not think of you.
But I'll like the Spring because it is simply Spring
    As the thrushes do.

Charlotte Mew (1869–1928)

Water, water, everywhere

FROM *THE RIME OF THE ANCIENT MARINER*, PART II

The fair breeze blew, the white foam flew,
The furrow followed free;
We were the first that ever burst
Into that silent sea.

Down dropped the breeze, the sails dropped down,
'Twas sad as sad could be;
And we did speak only to break
The silence of the sea!

All in a hot and copper sky,
The bloody Sun, at noon,
Right up above the mast did stand,
No bigger than the Moon.

Day after day, day after day,
We stuck, nor breath nor motion;
As idle as a painted ship
Upon a painted ocean.

Water, water, everywhere,
And all the boards did shrink;
Water, water, everywhere,
Nor any drop to drink.

Samuel Taylor Coleridge (1772–1834)

The Speech of Silence

The solemn Sea of Silence lies between us;
   I know thou livest, and thou lovest me;
And yet I wish some white ship would come sailing
   Across the ocean, bearing word from thee.

The dead-calm awes me with its awful stillness.
   No anxious doubts or fears disturb my breast;
I only ask some little wave of language,
   To stir this vast infinitude of rest.

I am oppressed with this great sense of loving;
   So much I give, so much receive from thee,
Like subtle incense, rising from a censer,
   So floats the fragrance of thy love round me.

All speech is poor, and written words unmeaning;
   Yet such I ask, blown hither by some wind,
To give relief to this too perfect knowledge,
   The Silence so impresses on my mind.

How poor the love that needeth word or message,
   To banish doubt or nourish tenderness!
I ask them but to temper love's convictions
   The Silence all too fully doth express.

Too deep the language which the spirit utters;
   Too vast the knowledge which my soul hath stirred;
Send some white ship across the Sea of Silence
   And interrupt its utterance with a word.

Ella Wheeler Wilcox (1850–1919)

Meadowlarks

In the silver light after a storm,
Under dripping boughs of bright new green,
I take the low path to hear the meadowlarks
Alone and high-hearted as if I were a queen.

What have I to fear in life or death
Who have known three things: the kiss in the night,
The white flying joy when a song is born,
And meadowlarks whistling in silver light.

Sara Teasdale (1884–1933)

Sic Vita

Like to the falling of a Starre,
Or as the flights of Eagles are,
Or like the fresh spring's gawdy hew;
Or silver drops of morning dew,
Or like a wind that chafes the flood,
Or bubbles which on water stood:
Even such is man, whose borrowed light
Is streight called in, and paid to night.

The Wind blowes out, the Bubble dies;
The Spring entombd in Autumn lies;
The Dew dries up, the Starre is shot;
The Flight is past, and Man forgot.

Henry King (1592–1669)

All our town in peace awaits you

FROM *THE SONG OF HIAWATHA: HIAWATHA'S DEPARTURE*

O'er the water floating, flying,
Something in the hazy distance,
Something in the mists of morning,
Loomed and lifted from the water,
Now seemed floating, now seemed flying,
Coming nearer, nearer, nearer.
        * * * *

It was neither goose nor diver,
Neither pelican nor heron,
O'er the water floating, flying,
Through the shining mist of morning,
But a birch canoe with paddles,
Rising, sinking on the water,
Dripping, flashing in the sunshine;
        * * * *

Then the joyous Hiawatha
Cried aloud and spake in this wise:
'Beautiful is the sun, O strangers,
When you come so far to see us!
All our town in peace awaits you,
All our doors stand open for you;
You shall enter all our wigwams,
For the heart's right hand we give you.
 'Never bloomed the earth so gayly,
Never shone the sun so brightly,

As to-day they shine and blossom
When you come so far to see us!
Never was our lake so tranquil,
Nor so free from rocks, and sand-bars;
For your birch canoe in passing
Has removed both rock and sand-bar.

* * * *

   Then the generous Hiawatha
Led the strangers to his wigwam,
Seated them on skins of bison,
Seated them on skins of ermine,
And the careful old Nokomis
Brought them food in bowls of basswood,
Water brought in birchen dippers,
And the calumet, the peace-pipe,
Filled and lighted for their smoking.
   All the old men of the village,
All the warriors of the nation,
All the Jossakeeds, the Prophets,
The magicians, the Wabenos,
And the Medicine-men, the Medas,
Came to bid the strangers welcome;
'It is well', they said, 'O brothers,
That you come so far to see us!'

Henry Wadsworth Longfellow (1807–1882)

A Poison Tree

I was angry with my friend;
I told my wrath, my wrath did end.
I was angry with my foe:
I told it not, my wrath did grow.

And I waterd it in fears,
Night & morning with my tears:
And I sunned it with smiles,
And with soft deceitful wiles.

And it grew both day and night.
Till it bore an apple bright.
And my foe beheld it shine,
And he knew that it was mine.

And into my garden stole,
When the night had veild the pole;
In the morning glad I see;
My foe outstretchd beneath the tree.

William Blake (1757–1827)

At the Mid Hour of Night

At the mid hour of night, when stars are weeping, I fly
To the lone vale we loved, when life shone warm in thine
   eye;
And I think oft, if spirits can steal from the regions of air,
To revisit past scenes of delight, thou wilt come to me there,
And tell me our love is remembered even in the sky.

Then I sing the wild song 'twas once was such pleasure
   to hear,
When our voices commingling breathed, like one, on the
   ear;
And, as Echo far off through the vale my sad orison rolls,
I think, Oh my love! 'tis thy voice from the Kingdom of
   Souls,
Faintly answering still the notes that once were so dear.

Thomas Moore (1779–1852)

Young and Old

FROM *THE WATER BABIES*

When all the world is young, lad,
    And all the trees are green;
And every goose a swan, lad,
    And every lass a queen;
Then hey for boot and horse, lad,
    And round the world away;
Young blood must have its course, lad,
    And every dog his day.

When all the world is old, lad,
    And all the trees are brown;
And all the sport is stale, lad,
    And all the wheels run down;
Creep home, and take your place there,
    The spent and maimed among:
God grant you find one face there,
    You loved when all was young.

Charles Kingsley (1819–1875)

The Fly-Away Horse

EXTRACT

And the Fly-Away Horse seeks those far-away lands
   You little folk dream of at night—
Where candy-trees grow, and honey-brooks flow,
   And corn-fields with popcorn are white;
And the beasts in the wood are ever so good
   To children who visit them there—
What glory astride of a lion to ride,
   Or to wrestle around with a bear!
     The monkeys, they say:
     'Come on, let us play,'
   And they frisk in the cocoa-nut trees:
     While the parrots, that cling
     To the peanut-vines, sing
Or converse with comparative ease!

Off! scamper to bed—you shall ride him to-night!
   For, as soon as you've fallen asleep,
With a jubilant neigh he shall bear you away
   Over forest and hillside and deep!
But tell us, my dear, all you see and you hear
   In those beautiful lands over there,
Where the Fly-Away Horse wings his far-away course
   With the wee one consigned to his care.

Then grandma will cry
In amazement: 'Oh, my!'
And she'll think it could never be so;
And only we two
Shall know it is true—
You and I, little precious! shall know!

Eugene Field (1850–1895)

Over Hill, Over Dale

FROM *A MIDSUMMER NIGHT'S DREAM*, ACT II, SCENE I

Over hill, over dale,
  Thorough bush, thorough brier,
Over park, over pale,
  Thorough flood, thorough fire,
I do wander every where,
Swifter than the moon's sphere;
And I serve the Fairy Queen,
To dew her orbs upon the green:
The cowslips tall her pensioners be;
In their gold coats spots you see;
Those be rubies, fairy favours,
In those freckles live their savours:
I must go seek some dew-drops here
And hang a pearl in every cowslip's ear.
Farewell, thou lob of spirits: I'll be gone;
Our queen and all her elves come here anon.

William Shakespeare (1564–1616)

The Soldier

If I should die, think only this of me:
   That there's some corner of a foreign field
That is for ever England. There shall be
   In that rich earth a richer dust concealed;
A dust whom England bore, shaped, made aware,
   Gave, once, her flowers to love, her ways to roam;
A body of England's, breathing English air,
   Washed by the rivers, blest by suns of home.

And think, this heart, all evil shed away,
   A pulse in the eternal mind, no less
      Gives somewhere back the thoughts by England given;
Her sights and sounds; dreams happy as her day;
   And laughter, learnt of friends; and gentleness,
      In hearts at peace, under an English heaven.

Rupert Brooke (1887–1915)

I Remember, I Remember

I remember, I remember,
The house where I was born,
The little window where the sun
Came peeping in at morn;
He never came a wink too soon,
Nor brought too long a day,
But now, I often wish the night
Had borne my breath away!

I remember, I remember,
The roses, red and white,
The violets, and the lily-cups,
Those flowers made of light!
The lilacs where the robin built,
And where my brother set
The laburnum on his birthday,—
The tree is living yet!

I remember, I remember,
Where I was used to swing,
And thought the air must rush as fresh
To swallows on the wing;
My spirit flew in feathers then,
That is so heavy now,
And summer pools could hardly cool
The fever on my brow!

I remember, I remember,
The fir trees dark and high;
I used to think their slender tops
Were close against the sky:
It was a childish ignorance,
But now 'tis little joy
To know I'm farther off from Heav'n
Than when I was a boy.

Thomas Hood (1799–1845)

Sympathy

I know what the caged bird feels, alas!
  When the sun is bright on the upland slopes;
When the wind stirs soft through the springing grass,
And the river flows like a stream of glass;
  When the first bird sings and the first bud opes,
And the faint perfume from its chalice steals—
I know what the caged bird feels!

I know why the caged bird beats his wing
  Till its blood is red on the cruel bars;
For he must fly back to his perch and cling
When he fain would be on the bough a-swing;
  And a pain still throbs in the old, old scars
And they pulse again with a keener sting—
I know why he beats his wing!

I know why the caged bird sings, ah me,
  When his wing is bruised and his bosom sore,—
When he beats his bars and he would be free;
It is not a carol of joy or glee,
  But a prayer that he sends from his heart's deep core,
But a plea, that upward to Heaven he flings—
I know why the caged bird sings!

Paul Laurence Dunbar (1872–1906)

The Sunshine

EXTRACT

I love the sunshine everywhere—
  In wood, and field, and glen;
I love it in the busy haunts
  Of town-imprisoned men.

I love it, when it streameth in
  The humble cottage door,
And casts the chequered casement shade
  Upon the red-brick floor.

I love it, where the children lie
  Deep in the clovery grass,
To watch among the twining roots,
  The gold-green beetle pass.

I love it, on the breezy sea,
  To glance on sail and oar,
While the great waves, like molten glass,
  Come leaping to the shore.

I love it, on the mountain-tops,
  Where lies the thawless snow;
And half a kingdom, bathed in light,
  Lies stretching out below.

Oh! yes, I love the sunshine!
  Like kindness, or like mirth,
Upon a human countenance,
  Is sunshine on the earth.

Upon the earth—upon the sea;
  And through the crystal air,
Or piled-up-clouds—the gracious sun
  Is glorious everywhere!

Mary Botham Howitt (1799–1888)

Love is Enough

Love is enough: though the World be a-waning,
And the woods have no voice but the voice of
    complaining,
    Though the sky be too dark for dim eyes to discover
The gold-cups and daisies fair blooming thereunder;
Though the hills be held shadows, and the sea a dark
    wonder
    And this day draw a veil over all deeds passed over,
Yet their hands shall not tremble, their feet shall not
    falter;
The void shall not weary, the fear shall not alter
    These lips and these eyes of the loved and the lover.

William Morris (1834–1896)

False Poets and True

TO WORDSWORTH

Look how the lark soars upward and is gone,
Turning a spirit as he nears the sky!
His voice is heard, but body there is none
To fix the vague excursions of the eye.
So, poets' songs are with us, tho' they die
Obscured, and hid by death's oblivious shroud,
And Earth inherits the rich melody
Like raining music from the morning cloud.
Yet, few there be who pipe so sweet and loud
Their voices reach us through the lapse of space:
The noisy day is deafen'd by a crowd
Of undistinguished birds, a twittering race;
But only lark and nightingale forlorn
Fill up the silences of night and morn.

Thomas Hood (1799–1845)

Shall I compare thee to a summer's day?

SONNET XVIII

Shall I compare thee to a summer's day?
Thou art more lovely and more temperate.
Rough winds do shake the darling buds of May,
And summer's lease hath all too short a date.
Sometime too hot the eye of heaven shines,
And often is his gold complexion dimmed;
And every fair from fair sometime declines,
By chance or nature's changing course untrimmed;
But thy eternal summer shall not fade,
Nor lose possession of that fair thou ow'st,
Nor shall death brag thou wand'rest in his shade,
When in eternal lines to time thou grow'st.
   So long as men can breathe or eyes can see,
   So long lives this, and this gives life to thee.

William Shakespeare (1564–1616)

JUNE

Pleasure, Not in Haste

The Best Thing in the World

What's the best thing in the world?
June-rose by May-dew impearled;
Sweet south-wind, that means no rain;
Truth, not cruel to a friend;
Pleasure, not in haste to end;
Beauty, not self-decked and curled
Till its pride is over-plain;
Light, that never makes you wink;
Memory, that gives no pain;
Love, when, so, you're loved again.
What's the best thing in the world?
—Something out of it, I think.

Elizabeth Barrett Browning (1806–1861)

Ode to a Nightingale

EXTRACT

O, for a draught of vintage! that hath been
  Cooled a long age in the deep-delvèd earth,
Tasting of Flora and the country green,
  Dance, and Provençal song, and sunburnt mirth!
O for a beaker full of the warm South,
  Full of the true, the blushful Hippocrene,
    With beaded bubbles winking at the brim,
      And purple-stainèd mouth;
  That I might drink, and leave the world unseen,
    And with thee fade away into the forest dim.

John Keats (1795–1821)

Voices of the Air

But then there comes that moment rare
When, for no cause that I can find,
The little voices of the air
Sound above all the sea and wind.

The sea and wind do then obey
And sighing, sighing double notes
Of double basses, content to play
A droning chord for the little throats—

The little throats that sing and rise
Up into the light with lovely ease
And a kind of magical, sweet surprise
To hear and know themselves for these—

For these little voices: the bee, the fly,
The leaf that taps, the pod that breaks,
The breeze on the grass-tops bending by,
The shrill quick sound that the insect makes.

Katherine Mansfield (1888–1923)

Mine

O how my heart is beating as her name I keep repeating,
  And I drink up joy like wine:
O how my heart is beating as her name I keep repeating,
  For the lovely girl is mine!
She's rich, she's fair, beyond compare,
Of noble mind, serene and kind—
And how my heart is beating as her name I keep
  repeating,
  For the lovely girl is mine!

O how my heart is beating as her name I keep repeating,
  In a music soft and fine;
O how my heart is beating as her name I keep repeating,
  For the girl I love is mine.
She owns no lands, has no white hands,
Her lot is poor, her life obscure;—
Yet how my heart is beating as her name I keep repeating,
  For the girl I love is mine!

Dinah Maria Craik (1826–1887)

The Echoing Green

The Sun does arise,
And make happy the skies;
The merry bells ring
To welcome the Spring;
The skylark and thrush,
The birds of the bush,
Sing louder around
To the bells' cheerful sound,
While our sports shall be seen
On the Echoing Green.

Old John, with white hair,
Does laugh away care,
Sitting under the oak,
Among the old folk.
They laugh at our play,
And soon they all say:
'Such, such were the joys
When we all, girls and boys,
In our youth time were seen
On the Echoing Green.'

Till the little ones, weary,
No more can be merry;
The sun does descend,
And our sports have an end.
Round the laps of their mothers
Many sisters and brothers,
Like birds in their nest,
Are ready for rest,
And sports no more seen
On the darkening Green.

William Blake (1757–1827)

A Red, Red Rose

O my Luve's like a red, red rose
That's newly sprung in June:
O my Luve's like the melodie
That's sweetly played in tune.

As fair art thou, my bonnie lass,
So deep in luve am I;
And I will luve thee still, my dear,
Till a' the seas gang dry.

Till a' the seas gang dry, my dear,
And the rocks melt wi' the sun;
I will love thee still, my dear,
While the sands o' life shall run.

And fare thee weel, my only luve!
And fare thee weel awhile!
And I will come again, my luve,
Tho' it were ten thousand mile!

Robert Burns (1759–1796)

To the Virgins, to Make Much of Time

Gather ye rosebuds while ye may,
   Old Time is still a-flying;
And this same flower that smiles today
   Tomorrow will be dying.

The glorious lamp of heaven, the sun,
   The higher he's a-getting,
The sooner will his race be run,
   And nearer he's to setting.

That age is best which is the first,
   When youth and blood are warmer;
But being spent, the worse, and worst
   Times still succeed the former.

Then be not coy, but use your time,
   And while ye may, go marry;
For having lost but once your prime,
   You may for ever tarry.

Robert Herrick (1591–1674)

On Marriage

FROM *THE PROPHET*

Love one another, but make not a bond of love:
   Let it rather be a moving sea between the shores of
   your souls.
      Fill each other's cup but drink not from one cup.
      Give one another of your bread but eat not from the
same loaf.
      Sing and dance together and be joyous, but let each
one of you be alone,
      Even as the strings of a lute are alone though they
quiver with the same music.

Give your hearts, but not into each other's keeping.
      For only the hand of Life can contain your hearts.
      And stand together yet not too near together:
      For the pillars of the temple stand apart,
      And the oak tree and the cypress grow not in each
other's shadow.

Kahlil Gibran (1883–1931)

Roses

FROM *THE SPANISH GYPSY*

You love the roses—so do I. I wish
The sky would rain down roses, as they rain
From off the shaken bush. Why will it not?
Then all the valley would be pink and white
And soft to tread on. They would fall as light
As feathers, smelling sweet; and it would be
Like sleeping and like waking, all at once!

George Eliot (1819–1880)

Sound Sleep

Some are laughing, some are weeping;
She is sleeping, only sleeping.
Round her rest wild flowers are creeping;
There the wind is heaping, heaping
Sweetest sweets of Summer's keeping,
By the cornfields ripe for reaping.

There are lilies, and there blushes
The deep rose, and there the thrushes
Sing till latest sunlight flushes
In the west; a fresh wind brushes
Through the leaves while evening hushes.

There by day the lark is singing
And the grass and weeds are springing:
There by night the bat is winging;
There forever winds are bringing
Far-off chimes of church-bells ringing.

Night and morning, noon and even,
Their sound fills her dreams with Heaven:
The long strife at length is striven:
Till her grave-bands shall be riven
Such is the good portion given
To her soul at rest and shriven.

Christina Rossetti (1830–1894)

Ode on Solitude

Happy the man, whose wish and care
  A few paternal acres bound,
Content to breathe his native air,
      In his own ground.

Whose herds with milk, whose fields with bread,
  Whose flocks supply him with attire,
Whose trees in summer yield him shade,
      In winter fire.

Blest, who can unconcern'dly find
  Hours, days, and years slide soft away,
In health of body, peace of mind,
      Quiet by day,

Sound sleep by night; study and ease,
  Together mixed; sweet recreation,
And innocence, which most does please,
      With meditation.

Thus let me live, unseen, unknown;
  Thus unlamented let me die;
Steal from the world, and not a stone
      Tell where I lie.

Alexander Pope (1688–1744)

Silence

Since I lost you I am silence-haunted,
  Sounds wave their little wings
A moment, then in weariness settle
  On the flood that soundless swings.

Whether the people in the street
  Like pattering ripples go by,
Or whether the theatre sighs and sighs
  With a loud, hoarse sigh:

Or the wind shakes a ravel of light
  Over the dead-black river,
Or night's last echoing
  Makes the daybreak shiver:

I feel the silence waiting
  To take them all up again
In its vast completeness, enfolding
  The sound of men.

D. H. Lawrence (1885–1930)

The Treasure

When colour goes home into the eyes,
   And lights that shine are shut again,
With dancing girls and sweet bird's cries
   Behind the gateways of the brain;
And that no-place which gave them birth, shall close
The rainbow and the rose:—

Still may Time hold some golden space
   Where I'll unpack that scented store
Of song and flower and sky and face,
   And count, and touch, and turn them o'er,
Musing upon them: as a mother, who
Has watched her children all the rich day through,
Sits, quiet-handed, in the fading light,
When children sleep, ere night.

Rupert Brooke (1887–1915)

I stood tip-toe upon a little hill

EXTRACT

I stood tip-toe upon a little hill,
The air was cooling, and so very still,
That the sweet buds which with a modest pride
Pull droopingly, in slanting curve aside,
Their scantly leaved, and finely tapering stems,
Had not yet lost those starry diadems
Caught from the early sobbing of the morn.
The clouds were pure and white as flocks new shorn,
And fresh from the clear brook; sweetly they slept
On the blue fields of heaven, and then there crept
A little noiseless noise among the leaves,
Born of the very sigh that silence heaves:
For not the faintest motion could be seen
Of all the shades that slanted o'er the green.
         * * * *

O'erhead we see the jasmine and sweet briar,
And bloomy grapes laughing from green attire;
While at our feet, the voice of crystal bubbles
Charms us at once away from all our troubles:
So that we feel uplifted from the world,
Walking upon the white clouds wreath'd and curl'd.

John Keats (1795–1821)

An hour with thee

An hour with thee!—When earliest day
Dapples with gold the eastern grey,
Oh, what can frame my mind to bear
The toil and turmoil, cark and care,
New griefs, which coming hours unfold,
And sad remembrance of the old?
   One hour with thee.

One hour with thee!—When burning June
Waves his red flag at pitch of noon;
What shall repay the faithful swain,
His labour on the sultry plain;
And more than cave or sheltering bough,
Cool feverish blood, and throbbing brow?
   One hour with thee.

One hour with thee!—When sun is set,
Oh, what can teach me to forget
The thankless labours of the day;
The hopes, the wishes, flung away;
The increasing wants, and lessening gains,
The master's pride, who scorns my pains?
   One hour with thee.

Sir Walter Scott (1771–1832)

In the Valley of Cauteretz

All along the valley, stream that flashest white,
Deepening thy voice with the deepening of the night,
All along the valley, where thy waters flow,
I walked with one I loved two and thirty years ago.
All along the valley, while I walked to-day,
The two and thirty years were a mist that rolls away;
For all along the valley, down thy rocky bed,
Thy living voice to me was as the voice of the dead,
And all along the valley, by rock and cave and tree,
The voice of the dead was a living voice to me.

Alfred, Lord Tennyson (1809–1892)

Roads

I know a country laced with roads,
They join the hills and they span the brooks,
They weave like a shuttle between broad fields,
And slide discreetly through hidden nooks.
They are canopied like a Persian dome
And carpeted with orient dyes.
They are myriad-voiced, and musical,
And scented with happiest memories.
O Winding roads that I know so well,
Every twist and turn, every hollow and hill!
They are set in my heart to a pulsing tune
Gay as a honey-bee humming in June.
'Tis the rhythmic beat of a horse's feet
And the pattering paws of a sheep-dog bitch;
'Tis the creaking trees, and the singing breeze,
And the rustle of leaves in the road-side ditch.

A cow in a meadow shakes her bell
And the notes cut sharp through the autumn air,
Each chattering brook bears a fleet of leaves
Their cargo the rainbow, and just now where
The sun splashed bright on the road ahead
A startled rabbit quivered and fled.
O Uphill roads and roads that dip down!
You curl your sun-spattered length along,
And your march is beaten into a song
By the softly ringing hoofs of a horse
And the panting breath of the dogs I love.
The pageant of Autumn follows its course
And the blue sky of Autumn laughs above.

And the song and the country become as one,
I see it as music, I hear it as light;
Prismatic and shimmering, trembling to tone,
The land of desire, my soul's delight.
And always it beats in my listening ears
With the gentle thud of a horse's stride,
With the swift-falling steps of many dogs,
Following, following at my side.
O Roads that journey to fairyland!
Radiant highways whose vistas gleam,
Leading me on, under crimson leaves,
To the opaline gates of the Castles of Dream.

Amy Lowell (1874–1925)

Come buy, come buy

FROM *GOBLIN MARKET*

Morning and evening
Maids heard the goblins cry:
'Come buy our orchard fruits,
Come buy, come buy:
Apples and quinces,
Lemons and oranges,
Plump unpecked cherries,
Melons and raspberries,
Bloom-down-cheeked peaches,
Swart-headed mulberries,
Wild free-born cranberries,
Crab-apples, dewberries,
Pine-apples, blackberries,
Apricots, strawberries;—
All ripe together
In summer weather,—
    * * * *

Sweet to tongue and sound to eye;
Come buy, come buy.'

Christina Rossetti (1830–1894)

Music, when soft voices die

Music, when soft voices die,
Vibrates in the memory—
Odours, when sweet violets sicken,
Live within the sense they quicken.

Rose leaves, when the rose is dead,
Are heaped for the belovèd's bed;
And so thy thoughts, when thou art gone,
Love itself shall slumber on.

Percy Bysshe Shelley (1792–1822)

Ducks' Ditty

FROM *THE WIND IN THE WILLOWS*

All along the backwater,
Through the rushes tall,
Ducks are a-dabbling,
Up tails all!

Ducks' tails, drakes' tails,
Yellow feet a-quiver,
Yellow bills all out of sight
Busy in the river!

Slushy green undergrowth
Where the roach swim—
Here we keep our larder,
Cool and full and dim.

Every one for what he likes!
We like to be
Heads down, tails up,
Dabbling free!

High in the blue above
Swifts whirl and call—
We are down a-dabbling
Up tails all!

Kenneth Grahame (1859–1932)

Laughing Song

When the green woods laugh with the voice of joy,
And the dimpling stream runs laughing by;
When the air does laugh with our merry wit,
And the green hill laughs with the noise of it;

When the meadows laugh with lively green,
And the grasshopper laughs in the merry scene,
When Mary and Susan and Emily
With their sweet round mouths sing 'Ha, Ha He!'

When the painted birds laugh in the shade,
Where our table with cherries and nuts is spread:
Come live, and be merry, and join with me,
To sing the sweet chorus of 'Ha, Ha, He!'

William Blake (1757–1827)

The Temper of a Maid

The Swallow dives in yonder air,
The Robin sings with sweetest ease,
The Apple shines among the leaves,
The Leaf is dancing in the breeze;
The Butterfly's on a warm stone,
The Bee is suckled by a flower;
The Wasp's inside a ripe red plum,
The Ant has found his load this hour;
The Squirrel counts and hides his nuts,
The Stoat is on a scent that burns;
The Mouse is nibbling a young shoot,
The Rabbit sits beside his ferns;
The Snake has found a sunny spot,
The Frog and Snail a slimy shade;
But I can find no joy on earth,
All through the temper of a maid.

W. H. Davies (1871–1940)

The Table and the Chair

I

Said the Table to the Chair,
'You can hardly be aware,
'How I suffer from the heat,
'And from chilblains on my feet!
'If we took a little walk,
'We might have a little talk!
'Pray let us take the air!'
Said the Table to the Chair.

II

Said the Chair unto the Table,
'Now you know we are not able!
'How foolishly you talk,
'When you know we cannot walk!'
Said the Table, with a sigh,
'It can do no harm to try,
'I've as many legs as you,
'Why can't we walk on two?'

III

So they both went slowly down,
And walked about the town
With a cheerful bumpy sound,
As they toddled round and round.
And everybody cried,
As they hastened to their side,
'See! the Table and the Chair
'Have come out to take the air!'

IV

But in going down an alley,
To a castle in a valley,
They completely lost their way,
And wandered all the day,
Till, to see them safely back,
They paid a Ducky-quack,
And a Beetle, and a Mouse,
Who took them to their house.

V

Then they whispered to each other,
'O delightful little brother!
'What a lovely walk we've taken!
'Let us dine on Beans and Bacon!'
So the Ducky, and the leetle
Browny-Mousy and the Beetle
Dined, and danced upon their heads
Till they toddled to their beds.

Edward Lear (1812–1888)

When I Am Dead, My Dearest

When I am dead, my dearest,
  Sing no sad songs for me;
Plant thou no roses at my head,
  Nor shady cypress tree:
Be the green grass above me
  With showers and dewdrops wet;
And if thou wilt, remember,
  And if thou wilt, forget.

I shall not see the shadows,
  I shall not feel the rain;
I shall not hear the nightingale
  Sing on, as if in pain:
And dreaming through the twilight
  That doth not rise nor set,
Haply I may remember,
  And haply may forget.

Christina Rossetti (1830–1894)

Dusk in June

Evening, and all the birds
  In a chorus of shimmering sound
Are easing their hearts of joy
  For miles around.

The air is blue and sweet,
  The few first stars are white,—
Oh let me like the birds
  Sing before night.

Sara Teasdale (1884–1933)

A Boy's Song

Where the pools are bright and deep,
Where the grey trout lies asleep,
Up the river and over the lea,
That's the way for Billy and me.

Where the blackbird sings the latest,
Where the hawthorn blooms the sweetest,
Where the nestlings chirp and flee,
That's the way for Billy and me.

Where the mowers mow the cleanest,
Where the hay lies thick and greenest,
There to track the homeward bee,
That's the way for Billy and me.

Where the hazel bank is steepest,
Where the shadow falls the deepest,
Where the clustering nuts fall free,
That's the way for Billy and me.

Why the boys should drive away
Little sweet maidens from the play,
Or love to banter and fight so well,
That's the thing I never could tell.

But this I know, I love to play
Through the meadow, among the hay;
Up the water and over the lea,
That's the way for Billy and me.

James Hogg (1770–1835)

Mutability

We are as clouds that veil the midnight moon;
How restlessly they speed, and gleam and quiver,
Streaking the darkness radiantly!—yet soon
Night closes round, and they are lost for ever:

Or like forgotten lyres, whose dissonant strings
Give various response to each varying blast,
To whose frail frame no second motion brings
One mood or modulation like the last.

We rest—A dream has power to poison sleep;
We rise—One wandering thought pollutes the day;
We feel, conceive or reason, laugh or weep;
Embrace fond woe, or cast our cares away:

It is the same!—For, be it joy or sorrow,
The path of its departure still is free:
Man's yesterday may ne'er be like his morrow;
Nought may endure but Mutability.

Percy Bysshe Shelley (1792–1822)

Eternity

He who binds to himself a joy
Does the winged life destroy
He who kisses the joy as it flies
Lives in eternity's sun rise

William Blake (1757–1827)

Adlestrop

Yes. I remember Adlestrop—
The name, because one afternoon
Of heat the express-train drew up there
Unwontedly. It was late June.

The steam hissed. Someone cleared his throat.
No one left and no one came
On the bare platform. What I saw
Was Adlestrop—only the name

And willows, willow-herb, and grass,
And meadowsweet, and haycocks dry,
No whit less still and lonely fair
Than the high cloudlets in the sky.

And for that minute a blackbird sang
Close by, and round him, mistier,
Farther and farther, all the birds
Of Oxfordshire and Gloucestershire.

Edward Thomas (1878–1917)

Dover Beach

The sea is calm tonight.
The tide is full, the moon lies fair
Upon the straits;—on the French coast the light
Gleams and is gone; the cliffs of England stand,
Glimmering and vast, out in the tranquil bay.
Come to the window, sweet is the night-air!
Only, from the long line of spray
Where the sea meets the moon-blanched land,
Listen! you hear the grating roar
Of pebbles which the waves draw back, and fling,
At their return, up the high strand,
Begin, and cease, and then again begin,
With tremulous cadence slow, and bring
The eternal note of sadness in.

Sophocles long ago
Heard it on the Ægean, and it brought
Into his mind the turbid ebb and flow
Of human misery; we
Find also in the sound a thought,
Hearing it by this distant northern sea.

The Sea of Faith
Was once, too, at the full, and round earth's shore
Lay like the folds of a bright girdle furled.
But now I only hear
Its melancholy, long withdrawing roar,
Retreating, to the breath
Of the night-wind, down the vast edges drear
And naked shingles of the world.

Ah, love, let us be true
To one another! for the world, which seems
To lie before us like a land of dreams,
So various, so beautiful, so new,
Hath really neither joy, nor love, nor light,
Nor certitude, nor peace, nor help for pain;
And we are here as on a darkling plain
Swept with confused alarms of struggle and flight,
Where ignorant armies clash by night.

Matthew Arnold (1822–1888)

JULY

Up, Up, the Long Delirious Burning Blue

The Garden

EXTRACT

What wondrous life in this I lead!
Ripe apples drop about my head;
The luscious clusters of the vine
Upon my mouth do crush their wine;
The nectarine and curious peach
Into my hands themselves do reach;
Stumbling on melons, as I pass,
Insnared with flowers, I fall on grass.

Meanwhile the mind, from pleasure less,
Withdraws into its happiness;
The mind, that ocean where each kind
Does straight its own resemblance find,
Yet it creates, transcending these,
Far other worlds, and other seas;
Annihilating all that's made
To a green thought in a green shade.

Andrew Marvell (1621–1678)

The Owl and the Pussy-Cat

The Owl and the Pussy-cat went to sea
  In a beautiful pea-green boat,
They took some honey, and plenty of money,
  Wrapped up in a five-pound note.
The Owl looked up to the stars above,
  And sang to a small guitar,
'O lovely Pussy! O Pussy, my love,
    What a beautiful Pussy you are,
        You are,
        You are!
What a beautiful Pussy you are!'

Pussy said to the Owl, 'You elegant fowl!
  How charmingly sweet you sing!
O let us be married! too long we have tarried:
  But what shall we do for a ring?'
They sailed away, for a year and a day,
  To the land where the Bong-Tree grows
And there in a wood a Piggy-wig stood
  With a ring at the end of his nose,
      His nose,
      His nose,
  With a ring at the end of his nose.

'Dear Pig, are you willing to sell for one shilling
   Your ring?' Said the Piggy, 'I will.'
So they took it away, and were married next day
   By the Turkey who lives on the hill.
They dined on mince, and slices of quince,
   Which they ate with a runcible spoon;
And hand in hand, on the edge of the sand,
   They danced by the light of the moon,
            The moon,
            The moon,
They danced by the light of the moon.

Edward Lear (1812–1888)

One Old Oxford Ox

One old Oxford ox opening oysters;
Two tee-totums totally tired of trying to trot to Tadbury;
Three tall tigers tippling tenpenny tea;
Four fat friars fanning fainting flies;
Five frippy Frenchmen foolishly fishing for flies;
Six sportsmen shooting snipes;
Seven Severn salmons swallowing shrimps;
Eight Englishmen eagerly examining Europe;
Nine nimble noblemen nibbling nonpareils;
Ten tinkers tinkling upon ten tin tinderboxes with ten
    tenpenny tacks;
Eleven elephants elegantly equipt;
Twelve typographical topographers typically translating
    types.

Anon

The Land of Counterpane

When I was sick and lay a-bed,
I had two pillows at my head,
And all my toys beside me lay
To keep me happy all the day.

And sometimes for an hour or so
I watched my leaden soldiers go,
With different uniforms and drills,
Among the bed-clothes, through the hills.

And sometimes sent my ships in fleets
All up and down among the sheets;
Or brought my trees and houses out,
And planted cities all about.

I was the giant great and still
That sits upon the pillow-hill,
And sees before him, dale and plain
The pleasant land of counterpane.

Robert Louis Stevenson (1850–1894)

Sudden Light

I have been here before,
But when or how I cannot tell:
I know the grass beyond the door,
The sweet keen smell,
The sighing sound, the lights around the shore.

You have been mine before,—
How long ago I may not know:
But just when at that swallow's soar
Your neck turn'd so,
Some veil did fall,—I knew it all of yore.

Has this been thus before?
And shall not thus time's eddying flight
Still with our lives our love restore
In death's despite,
And day and night yield one delight once more?

Dante Gabriel Rossetti (1828–1882)

The School Boy

I love to rise in a summer morn,
When the birds sing on every tree;
The distant huntsman winds his horn,
And the skylark sings with me:
O! what sweet company.

But to go to school in a summer morn,—
O! It drives all joy away;
Under a cruel eye outworn,
The little ones spend the day
In sighing and dismay.

Ah! then at times I drooping sit,
And spend many an anxious hour;
Nor in my book can I take delight,
Nor sit in learning's bower,
Worn thro' with dreary shower.

How can the bird that is born for joy
Sit in a cage and sing?
How can a child, when fears annoy,
But droop his tender wing,
And forget his youthful spring?

O! father and mother if buds are nipped,
And blossoms blown away;
And if the tender plants are stripped
Of their joy in the springing day,
By sorrow and care's dismay,—

How shall the summer arise in joy,
Or the summer fruits appear?
Or how shall we gather what griefs destroy,
Or bless the mellowing year,
When the blasts of winter appear?

William Blake (1757–1827)

The Lake Isle of Innisfree

I will arise and go now, and go to Innisfree,
And a small cabin build there, of clay and wattles made:
Nine bean-rows will I have there, a hive for the honey-bee;
And live alone in the bee-loud glade.

And I shall have some peace there, for peace comes
   dropping slow,
Dropping from the veils of the morning to where the
   cricket sings;
There midnight's all a glimmer, and noon a purple glow,
And evening full of the linnet's wings.

I will arise and go now, for always night and day
I hear lake water lapping with low sounds by the shore;
While I stand on the roadway, or on the pavements grey,
I hear it in the deep heart's core.

W. B. Yeats (1865–1939)

The Poplar Field

The poplars are felled, farewell to the shade,
And the whispering sound of the cool colonnade;
The winds play no longer and sing in the leaves,
Nor Ouse on his bosom their image receives.

Twelve years have elaps'd since I last took a view
Of my favourite field and the bank where they grew;
And now in the grass behold they are laid,
And the tree is my seat, that once lent me a shade.

The blackbird has fled to another retreat,
Where the hazels afford him a screen from the heat,
And the scene where his melody charm'd me before,
Resounds with his sweet-flowing ditty no more.

My fugitive years are hasting away,
And I must ere long lie as lowly as they,
With a turf on my breast and a stone at my head,
Ere another such grove shall arise in its stead.

The change both my heart and my fancy employs;
I reflect on the frailty of man and his joys:
Short-lived as we are, yet our pleasures, we see,
Have a still shorter date, and die sooner than we.

William Cowper (1731–1800)

Be not afeard. The isle is full of noises

FROM *THE TEMPEST*, ACT III, SCENE II

Be not afeard. The isle is full of noises,
Sounds, and sweet airs, that give delight and hurt not.
Sometimes a thousand twangling instruments
Will hum about mine ears, and sometime voices
That, if I then had waked after long sleep
Will make me sleep again; and then in dreaming
The clouds methought would open and show riches
Ready to drop upon me, that when I waked
I cried to dream again.

William Shakespeare (1564–1616)

The Waterfall

EXTRACT

With what deep murmurs through time's silent stealth
Doth thy transparent, cool, and watery wealth
  Here flowing fall,
  And chide, and call,
As if his liquid, loose retinue stayed
Lingering, and were of this steep place afraid,
  The common pass
  Where, clear as glass,
  All must descend
  Not to an end,
But quickened by this deep and rocky grave,
Rise to a longer course more bright and brave.

Henry Vaughan (1621–1695)

Meeting at Night

The grey sea and the long black land;
And the yellow half-moon large and low;
And the startled little waves that leap
In fiery ringlets from their sleep,
As I gain the cove with pushing prow,
And quench its speed i' the slushy sand.

Then a mile of warm sea-scented beach;
Three fields to cross till a farm appears;
A tap at the pane, the quick sharp scratch
And blue spurt of a lighted match,
And a voice less loud, thro' its joys and fears,
Than the two hearts beating each to each!

Robert Browning (1812–1889)

And wilt thou have me fashion into speech

And wilt thou have me fashion into speech
The love I bear thee, finding words enough,
And hold the torch out, while the winds are rough,
Between our faces, to cast light on each?—
I drop it at thy feet. I cannot teach
My hand to hold my spirit so far off
From myself—me—that I should bring thee proof
In words, of love hid in me out of reach.
Nay, let the silence of my womanhood
Commend my woman-love to thy belief,—
Seeing that I stand unwon, however wooed,
And rend the garment of my life, in brief,
By a most dauntless, voiceless fortitude,
Lest one touch of this heart convey its grief.

Elizabeth Barrett Browning (1806–1861)

Composed a few miles above Tintern Abbey, on revisiting the banks of the Wye during a tour, July 13 1798

EXTRACT

For I have learned
To look on nature, not as in the hour
Of thoughtless youth, but hearing oftentimes
The still, sad music of humanity,
Nor harsh nor grating, though of ample power
To chasten and subdue. And I have felt
A presence that disturbs me with the joy
Of elevated thoughts; a sense sublime
Of something far more deeply interfused,
Whose dwelling is the light of setting suns,
And the round ocean, and the living air,
And the blue sky, and in the mind of man,
A motion and a spirit, that impels
All thinking things, all objects of all thought,
And rolls through all things. Therefore am I still
A lover of the meadows and the woods,
And mountains; and of all that we behold
From this green earth; of all the mighty world
Of eye and ear, both what they half-create,
And what perceive; well pleased to recognize
In nature and the language of the sense,
The anchor of my purest thoughts, the nurse,
The guide, the guardian of my heart, and soul
Of all my moral being.

William Wordsworth (1770–1850)

From My Diary, July 1914

Leaves
  Murmuring by miriads in the shimmering trees.
Lives
  Wakening with wonder in the Pyrenees.
Birds
  Cheerily chirping in the early day.
Bards
  Singing of summer, scything thro' the hay.
Bees
  Shaking the heavy dews from bloom and frond.
Boys
  Bursting the surface of the ebony pond.
Flashes
  Of swimmers carving thro' the sparkling cold.
Fleshes
  Gleaming with wetness to the morning gold.
A mead
  Bordered about with warbling water brooks.
A maid
  Laughing the love-laugh with me; proud of looks.
The heat
  Throbbing between the upland and the peak.
Her heart
  Quivering with passion to my pressed cheek.

Braiding

Of floating flames across the mountain brow.

Brooding

Of stillness; and a sighing of the bough.

Stirs

Of leaflets in the gloom; soft petal-showers;

Stars

Expanding with the starr'd nocturnal flowers.

Wilfred Owen (1893–1918)

We Sat at the Window

(BOURNEMOUTH, 1875)

We sat at the window looking out,
And the rain came down like silken strings
That Swithin's day. Each gutter and spout
Babbled unchecked in the busy way
   Of witless things:
Nothing to read, nothing to see
Seemed in that room for her and me
   On Swithin's day.

We were irked by the scene, by our own selves; yes,
For I did not know, nor did she infer
How much there was to read and guess
By her in me, and to see and crown
   By me in her.
Wasted were two souls in their prime,
And great was the waste, that July time
   When the rain came down.

Thomas Hardy (1840–1928)

One Art

The art of losing isn't hard to master;
so many things seem filled with the intent
to be lost that their loss is no disaster.

Lose something every day. Accept the fluster
of lost door keys, the hour badly spent.
The art of losing isn't hard to master.

Then practice losing farther, losing faster:
faces, and names, and where it was you meant
to travel. None of these will bring disaster.

I lost my mother's watch. And look! my last, or
next-to-last, of three loved houses went.
The art of losing isn't hard to master.

I lost two cities, lovely ones. And, vaster,
some realms I owned, two rivers, a continent.
I miss them, but it wasn't a disaster.

—Even losing you (the joking voice, a gesture
I love) I shan't have lied. It's evident
the art of losing's not too hard to master
though it may look like *(Write it!)* like disaster.

Elizabeth Bishop (1911–1979)

Love's Philosophy

The fountains mingle with the river
And the rivers with the Ocean,
The winds of Heaven mix for ever
With a sweet emotion;
Nothing in the world is single;
All things by a law divine
In one spirit meet and mingle.
Why not I with thine?—

See the mountains kiss high Heaven
And the waves clasp one another;
No sister-flower would be forgiven
If it disdained its brother;
And the sunlight clasps the earth
And the moonbeams kiss the sea:
What is all this sweet work worth
If thou kiss not me?

Percy Bysshe Shelley (1792–1822)

Song of the Brook

FROM *THE BROOK: AN IDYL*

I come from haunts of coot and hern,
   I make a sudden sally
And sparkle out among the fern,
   To bicker down a valley.

By thirty hills I hurry down,
   Or slip between the ridges,
By twenty thorpes, a little town,
   And half a hundred bridges.

Till last by Philip's farm I flow
   To join the brimming river,
For men may come and men may go,
   But I go on for ever.

I chatter over stony ways,
   In little sharps and trebles,
I bubble into eddying bays,
   I babble on the pebbles.

With many a curve my banks I fret
   By many a field and fallow,
And many a fairy foreland set
   With willow-weed and mallow.

I chatter, chatter, as I flow
   To join the brimming river,
For men may come and men may go,
   But I go on for ever.

I wind about, and in and out,
   With here a blossom sailing,
And here and there a lusty trout,
   And here and there a grayling,

And here and there a foamy flake
   Upon me, as I travel
With many a silvery waterbreak
   Above the golden gravel,

And draw them all along, and flow
   To join the brimming river
For men may come and men may go,
   But I go on for ever.

I steal by lawns and grassy plots,
   I slide by hazel covers;
I move the sweet forget-me-nots
   That grow for happy lovers.

I slip, I slide, I gloom, I glance,
  Among my skimming swallows;
I make the netted sunbeam dance
  Against my sandy shallows.

I murmur under moon and stars
  In brambly wildernesses;
I linger by my shingly bars;
  I loiter round my cresses;

And out again I curve and flow
  To join the brimming river,
For men may come and men may go,
  But I go on for ever.

Alfred, Lord Tennyson (1809–1892)

The Fairies

EXTRACT

Up the airy mountain,
  Down the rushy glen,
We daren't go a-hunting
  For fear of little men;
Wee folk, good folk,
  Trooping all together;
Green jacket, red cap,
  And white owl's feather!

Down along the rocky shore
  Some make their home,
They live on crispy pancakes
  Of yellow tide-foam;
Some in the reeds
  Of the black mountain lake,
With frogs for their watch-dogs,
  All night awake.

Up the airy mountain,
  Down the rushy glen,
We daren't go a-hunting
  For fear of little men;
Wee folk, good folk,
  Trooping all together;
Green jacket, red cap,
  And white owl's feather!

William Allingham (1824–1889)

A wet sheet and a flowing sea

A wet sheet and a flowing sea,
  A wind that follows fast
And fills the white and rustling sail
  And bends the gallant mast;
And bends the gallant mast, my boys,
  While like the eagle free
Away the good ship flies, and leaves
  Old England on the lee.

'O for a soft and gentle wind!'
  I heard a fair one cry:
But give to me the snoring breeze
  And white waves heaving high;
And white waves heaving high, my lads,
  The good ship tight and free—
The world of waters is our home,
  And merry men are we.

There's tempest in yon hornèd moon,
  And lightning in yon cloud:
But hark the music, mariners!
  The wind is piping loud;
The wind is piping loud, my boys,
  The lightning flashes free—
While the hollow oak our palace is,
  Our heritage the sea.

Allan Cunningham (1784–1842)

John Anderson my jo

John Anderson my jo, John,
　　When we were first acquent;
Your locks were like the raven,
　　Your bonie brow was brent;
But now your brow is beld, John,
　　Your locks are like the snow;
But blessings on your frosty pow,
　　John Anderson my jo.

John Anderson my jo, John,
　　We clamb the hill thegither;
And mony a canty day, John,
　　We've had wi' ane anither:
Now we maun totter down, John,
And hand in hand we'll go,
And sleep thegither at the foot,
John Anderson my jo.

Robert Burns (1759–1796)

Crossing the Bar

Sunset and evening star,
    And one clear call for me!
And may there be no moaning of the bar,
    When I put out to sea,

But such a tide as moving seems asleep,
    Too full for sound and foam,
When that which drew from out the boundless deep
    Turns again home.

Twilight and evening bell,
    And after that the dark!
And may there be no sadness of farewell,
    When I embark;

For tho' from out our bourne of Time and Place
    The flood may bear me far,
I hope to see my Pilot face to face,
    When I have crost the bar.

Alfred, Lord Tennyson (1809–1892)

High Flight

Oh! I have slipped the surly bonds of Earth
And danced the skies on laughter-silvered wings;
Sunward I've climbed, and joined the tumbling mirth
of sun-split clouds,—and done a hundred things
You have not dreamed of—wheeled and soared and swung
High in the sunlit silence. Hov'ring there,
I've chased the shouting wind along, and flung
My eager craft through footless halls of air ...

Up, up the long, delirious, burning blue
I've topped the wind-swept heights with easy grace
Where never lark or even eagle flew—
And, while with silent lifting mind I've trod
The high untrespassed sanctity of space,
Put out my hand, and touched the face of God.

John Gillespie Magee Jr. (1922–1941)

The Distance

Over the sounding sea,
Off the wandering sea
I smelt the smell of the distance
And longed for another existence.
Smell of pineapple, maize, and myrrh,
Parrot-feather and monkey-fur,
   Brown spice,
   Blue ice,
Fields of tobacco and tea and rice,

And soundless snows,
And snowy cotton,
Otto of rose
Incense in an ivory palace,
Jungle rivers rich and rotten,
   Slumbering valleys
   Smouldering mountains
   Rank morasses
   And frozen fountains,
Black molasses and purple wine,
Coral and pearl and tar and brine,
The smell of panther and polar-bear
   And leopard-lair
   And mermaid-hair
Came from the four-cornered distance,
And I longed for another existence.

Eleanor Farjeon (1881–1965)

I Saw a Ship A-Sailing

I saw a ship a-sailing,
  A-sailing on the sea;
And, oh! it was all laden
  With pretty things for thee!

There were comfits in the cabin,
  And apples in the hold;
The sails were made of silk,
  And the masts were made of gold:

The four-and-twenty sailors,
  That stood between the decks,
Were four-and-twenty white mice,
  With chains about their necks.

The captain was a duck,
  With a packet on his back;
And when the ship began to move,
  The captain said, 'Quack! quack!'

Anon

A London Plane-Tree

Green is the plane-tree in the square,
  The other trees are brown;
They droop and pine for country air;
  The plane-tree loves the town.

Here from my garret-pane, I mark
  The plane-tree bud and blow,
Shed her recuperative bark,
  And spread her shade below.

Among her branches, in and out,
  The city breezes play;
The dun fog wraps her round about;
  Above, the smoke curls grey.

Others the country take for choice,
  And hold the town in scorn;
But she has listened to the voice
  On city breezes borne.

Amy Levy (1861–1889)

The Song of Wandering Aengus

I went out to the hazel wood,
Because a fire was in my head,
And cut and peeled a hazel wand,
And hooked a berry to a thread;
And when white moths were on the wing,
And moth-like stars were flickering out,
I dropped the berry in a stream
And caught a little silver trout.

When I had laid it on the floor
I went to blow the fire a-flame,
But something rustled on the floor,
And some one called me by my name:
It had become a glimmering girl
With apple blossom in her hair
Who called me by my name and ran
And faded through the brightening air.

Though I am old with wandering,
Through hollow lands and hilly lands,
I will find out where she has gone,
And kiss her lips and take her hands;
And walk among long dappled grass,
And pluck till time and times are done
The silver apples of the moon,
The golden apples of the sun.

W. B. Yeats (1865–1939)

Fairy Song

EXTRACT

The moonlight fades from flower and tree,
  And the stars dim one by one;
The tale is told, the song is sung,
  And the Fairy feast is done.
The night-wind rocks the sleeping flowers,
  And sings to them, soft and low.
The early birds erelong will wake:
  'Tis time for the Elves to go.

From bird, and blossom, and bee,
  We learn the lessons they teach;
And seek, by kindly deeds, to win
  A loving friend in each.
And though unseen on earth we dwell,
  Sweet voices whisper low,
And gentle hearts most joyously greet
  The Elves where'er they go.

When next we meet in the Fairy dell,
  May the silver moon's soft light
Shine then on faces gay as now,
  And Elfin hearts as light.
Now spread each wing, for the eastern sky
  With sunlight soon will glow.
The morning star shall light us home:
  Farewell! for the Elves must go.

Louisa May Alcott (1832–1888)

The Windhover

TO CHRIST OUR LORD

I caught this morning morning's minion, king-
　dom of daylight's dauphin, dapple-dawn-drawn Falcon,
　in his riding
　Of the rolling level underneath him steady air, and
　striding
High there, how he rung upon the rein of a wimpling wing
In his ecstasy! then off, off forth on swing,
　As a skate's heel sweeps smooth on a bow-bend: the
　hurl and gliding
　Rebuffed the big wind. My heart in hiding
Stirred for a bird,—the achieve of, the mastery of the
　thing!

Brute beauty and valour and act, oh, air, pride, plume, here
　Buckle! AND the fire that breaks from thee then, a
　billion
Times told lovelier, more dangerous, O my chevalier!

　No wonder of it: shéer plód makes plough down sillion
Shine, and blue-bleak embers, ah my dear,
　Fall, gall themselves, and gash gold-vermilion.

Gerard Manley Hopkins (1844–1889)

Home From Abroad

Far-fetched with tales of other worlds and ways,
My skin well-oiled with wines of the Levant,
I set my face into a filial smile
To greet the pale, domestic kiss of Kent.

But shall I never learn? That gawky girl,
Recalled so primly in my foreign thoughts,
Becomes again the green-haired queen of love
Whose wanton form dilates as it delights.

Her rolling tidal landscape floods the eye
And drowns Chianti in a dusky stream;
The flower-flecked grasses swim with simple horses,
The hedges choke with roses fat as cream.

So do I breathe the hayblown airs of home,
And watch the sea-green elms drip birds and shadows,
And as the twilight nets the plunging sun
My heart's keel slides to rest among the meadows.

Laurie Lee (1914–1997)

Summer Song of the Strawberry-Girl

It is summer! it is summer! how beautiful it looks!
There is sunshine on the old gray hills, and sunshine on
   the brooks
A singing-bird on every bough, soft perfumes on the air,
A happy smile on each young lip, and gladness everywhere.

Oh! is it not a pleasant thing to wander through the woods,
To look upon the painted flowers, and watch the opening
   buds;
Or seated in the deep cool shade at some tall ash-tree's
   root,
To fill my little basket with the sweet and scented fruit?

They tell me that my father's poor—that is no grief to me
When such a blue and brilliant sky my upturn'd eye can see;
They tell me, too, that richer girls can sport with toy and
   gem;
It may be so—and yet, methinks, I do not envy them.

When forth I go upon my way, a thousand toys are mine,
The clusters of dark violets, the wreaths of the wild vine;
My jewels are the primrose pale, the bind-weed, and the
   rose;
And shew me any courtly gem more beautiful than those.

And then the fruit! the glowing fruit, how sweet the scent
it breathes!
I love to see its crimson cheek rest on the bright green
leaves!
Summer's own gift of luxury, in which the poor may share,
The wild-wood fruit my eager eye is seeking everywhere.

Oh! summer is a pleasant time, with all its sounds and
sights;
Its dewy mornings, balmy eves, and tranquil calm delights;
I sigh when first I see the leaves fall yellow on the plain,
And all the winter long I sing—Sweet summer, come
again.

Mary Botham Howitt (1799–1888)

AUGUST

Luminous Grasses, and the Merry Sun

Rich music breathes in Summer's every sound

FROM *SUMMER IMAGES*

Rich music breathes in Summer's every sound;
   And in her harmony of varied greens,
Woods, meadows, hedge-rows, corn-fields, all around
   Much beauty intervenes,
Filling with harmony the ear and eye;
   While o'er the mingling scenes
    Far spreads the laughing sky.

John Clare (1793–1864)

Barter

Life has loveliness to sell,
All beautiful and splendid things,
Blue waves whitened on a cliff,
Soaring fire that sways and sings,
And children's faces looking up
Holding wonder like a cup.

Life has loveliness to sell,
Music like a curve of gold,
Scent of pine trees in the rain,
Eyes that love you, arms that hold,
And for your spirit's still delight,
Holy thoughts that star the night.

Spend all you have for loveliness,
Buy it and never count the cost;
For one white singing hour of peace
Count many a year of strife well lost,
And for a breath of ecstasy
Give all you have been, or could be.

Sara Teasdale (1884–1933)

Sound, sound the clarion

FROM *THE CALL*

Sound, sound the clarion, fill the fife!
Throughout the sensual world proclaim,
One crowded hour of glorious life
Is worth an age without a name.

Thomas Osbert Mordaunt (1730–1809)

i thank You God for most this amazing

i thank You God for most this amazing
day: for the leaping greenly spirits of trees
and a blue true dream of sky; and for everything
which is natural which is infinite which is yes

(i who have died am alive again today,
and this is the sun's birthday; this is the birth
day of life and of love and wings: and of the gay
great happening illimitably earth)

how should tasting touching hearing seeing
breathing any—lifted from the no
of all nothing—human merely being
doubt unimaginable You?

(now the ears of my ears awake and
now the eyes of my eyes are opened)

e.e. cummings (1894–1962)

They are not long

They are not long, the weeping and the laughter,
  Love and desire and hate:
I think they have no portion in us after
  We pass the gate.

They are not long, the days of wine and roses:
  Out of a misty dream
Our path emerges for a while, then closes
  Within a dream.

Ernest Dowson (1867–1900)

Sweet and low

SONG FROM *THE PRINCESS*

Sweet and low, sweet and low,
  Wind of the western sea,
Low, low, breathe and blow,
  Wind of the western sea!
Over the rolling waters go,
Come from the dying moon, and blow,
  Blow him again to me;
While my little one, while my pretty one, sleeps.

Alfred, Lord Tennyson (1809–1892)

Subway Wind

Far down, down through the city's great gaunt gut
    The gray train rushing bears the weary wind;
In the packed cars the fans the crowd's breath cut,
    Leaving the sick and heavy air behind.
And pale-cheeked children seek the upper door
    To give their summer jackets to the breeze;
Their laugh is swallowed in the deafening roar
    Of captive wind that moans for fields and seas;
Seas cooling warm where native schooners drift
    Through sleepy waters, while gulls wheel and sweep,
Waiting for windy waves the keels to lift
    Lightly among the islands of the deep;
Islands of lofty palm trees blooming white
    That lend their perfume to the tropic sea,
Where fields lie idle in the dew-drenched night,
    And the Trades float above them fresh and free.

Claude McKay (1889–1948)

Afternoon Service at Mellstock

On afternoons of drowsy calm
    We stood in the panelled pew,
Singing one-voiced a Tate-and-Brady psalm
    To the tune of 'Cambridge New.'

We watched the elms, we watched the rooks,
    The clouds upon the breeze,
Between the whiles of glancing at our books,
    And swaying like the trees.

So mindless were those outpourings!—
    Though I am not aware
That I have gained by subtle thought on things
    Since we stood psalming there.

Thomas Hardy (1840–1928)

O Captain! My Captain!

O Captain! my Captain! our fearful trip is done,
The ship has weather'd every rack, the prize we sought is won,
The port is near, the bells I hear, the people all exulting,
While follow eyes the steady keel, the vessel grim and daring;
  But O heart! heart! heart!
    O the bleeding drops of red,
      Where on the deck my Captain lies,
        Fallen cold and dead.

O Captain! my Captain! rise up and hear the bells;
Rise up—for you the flag is flung—for you the bugle trills,
For you bouquets and ribbon'd wreaths—for you the shores a-crowding,
For you they call, the swaying mass, their eager faces turning;
  Here Captain! dear father!
    his arm beneath your head!
      It is some dream that on the deck,
        You've fallen cold and dead.

My Captain does not answer, his lips are pale and still,
My father does not feel my arm, he has no pulse nor will,
The ship is anchor'd safe and sound, its voyage closed and done,
From fearful trip the victor ship comes in with object won;
   Exult O shores, and ring O bells!
    But I with mournful tread,
      Walk the deck my Captain lies,
        Fallen cold and dead.

Walt Whitman (1819–1892)

Full of sound and fury, signifying nothing

FROM *MACBETH*, ACT V, SCENE V

Tomorrow, and tomorrow, and tomorrow,
Creeps in this petty pace from day to day,
To the last syllable of recorded time;
And all our yesterdays have lighted fools
The way to dusty death. Out, out, brief candle!
Life's but a walking shadow, a poor player,
That struts and frets his hour upon the stage,
And then is heard no more. It is a tale
Told by an idiot, full of sound and fury,
Signifying nothing.

William Shakespeare (1564–1616)

I Am

I am—yet what I am none cares or knows;
   My friends forsake me like a memory lost:—
I am the self-consumer of my woes;—
   They rise and vanish in oblivion's host,
Like shadows in love-frenzied stifled throes:—
And yet I am and live—like vapours tossed

Into the nothingness of scorn and noise,—
   Into the living sea of waking dreams,
Where there is neither sense of life or joys,
   But the vast shipwreck of my life's esteems;
Even the dearest that I loved the best
Are strange—nay, rather, stranger than the rest.

I long for scenes, where man hath never trod,
   A place where woman never smiled or wept,
There to abide with my Creator, God;
   And sleep as I in childhood, sweetly slept,
Untroubling, and untroubled where I lie,
The grass below—above the vaulted sky.

John Clare (1793–1864)

Love's Land

Oh, Love builds on the azure sea,
  And Love builds on the golden sand,
And Love builds on the rose-winged cloud,
  And sometimes Love builds on the land!

Oh, if Love build on sparkling sea,
  And if Love build on golden strand,
And if Love build on rosy cloud,
  To Love these are the solid land!

Oh, Love will build his lily walls,
  And Love his pearly roof will rear,
On cloud, or land, or mist, or sea—
  Love's solid land is everywhere!

Isabella Valancy Crawford (1850–1887)

No man is an island

FROM *DEVOTIONS UPON EMERGENT OCCASIONS*

No man is an island entire of itself; every man
is a piece of the continent, a part of the main.
If a clod be washed away by the sea, Europe
is the less, as well as if a promontory were, as
well as if a manor of thy friend's or of thine
own were; any man's death diminishes me,
because I am involved in mankind,
and therefore never send to know for whom
the bell tolls; it tolls for thee.

John Donne (1572–1631)

Long Island Sound

I see it as it looked one afternoon
In August,—by a fresh soft breeze o'erblown.
The swiftness of the tide, the light thereon,
A far-off sail, white as a crescent moon.
The shining waters with pale currents strewn,
The quiet fishing-smacks, the Eastern cove,
The semi-circle of its dark, green grove.
The luminous grasses, and the merry sun
In the grave sky; the sparkle far and wide,
Laughter of unseen children, cheerful chirp
Of crickets, and low lisp of rippling tide,
Light summer clouds fantastical as sleep
Changing unnoted while I gazed thereon.
All these fair sounds and sights I made my own.

Emma Lazarus (1849–1887)

The Sea Shell

FROM *THE EXCURSION*, BOOK IV

      'I have seen
A curious child, who dwelt upon a tract
Of inland ground, applying to his ear
The convolutions of a smooth-lipped shell;
To which, in silence hushed, his very soul
Listened intensely; and his countenance soon
Brightened with joy; for from within were heard
Murmurings, whereby the monitor expressed
Mysterious union with its native sea.
Even such a shell the universe itself
Is to the ear of Faith; and there are times,
I doubt not, when to you it doth impart
Authentic tidings of invisible things;
Of ebb and flow, and ever-during power;
And central peace, subsisting at the heart
Of endless agitation.'

William Wordsworth (1770–1850)

A Portable Paradise

And if I speak of Paradise,
then I'm thinking of my grandmother
who told me to carry it always
on my person, concealed, so
no one else would know it but me.
That way they can't steal it, she'd say.
And if life puts you under pressure,
trace its ridges in your pocket,
smell its piney scent on your handkerchief,
hum its anthem under your breath.
And if your stresses are sustained and daily,
get yourself to an empty room—be it hotel,
hostel or hovel—find a lamp
and empty your paradise onto a desk:
your white sands, green hills and fresh fish.
Shine the lamp on it like the fresh hope
of morning, and keep staring at it till you sleep.

Roger Robinson (b.1982)

Thy voice is on the rolling air

FROM *IN MEMORIAM A.H.H.*

Thy voice is on the rolling air;
  I hear thee where the waters run;
  Thou standest in the rising sun,
And in the setting thou art fair.
        * * * *

Far off thou art, but ever nigh;
  I have thee still, and I rejoice;
  I prosper, circled with thy voice;
I shall not lose thee tho' I die.

Alfred, Lord Tennyson (1809–1892)

Man was made for Joy & Woe

FROM *AUGURIES OF INNOCENCE*

It is right it should be so
Man was made for Joy & Woe
And when this we rightly know
Thro the World we safely go
Joy & Woe are woven fine
A Clothing for the soul divine
Under every grief & pine
Runs a joy with silken twine

William Blake (1757–1827)

It is a beauteous Evening, calm and free

It is a beauteous Evening, calm and free;
The holy time is quiet as a Nun
Breathless with adoration; the broad sun
Is sinking down in its tranquillity;
The gentleness of heaven broods o'er the Sea:
Listen! the mighty Being is awake
And doth with his eternal motion make
A sound like thunder—everlastingly.
Dear Child! dear Girl! that walkest with me here,
If thou appear'st untouched by solemn thought,
Thy nature is not therefore less divine:
Thou liest in Abraham's bosom all the year;
And worshipp'st at the Temple's inner shrine,
God being with thee when we know it not.

William Wordsworth (1770–1850)

The Habit of Perfection

EXTRACT

Elected Silence, sing to me
And beat upon my whorlèd ear,
Pipe me to pastures still and be
The music that I care to hear.

Shape nothing, lips; be lovely-dumb:
It is the shut, the curfew sent
From there where all surrenders come
Which only makes you eloquent.

Gerard Manley Hopkins (1844–1889)

These I have loved

FROM *THE GREAT LOVER*

These I have loved:
    White plates and cups, clean-gleaming,
Ringed with blue lines; and feathery, faery dust;
Wet roofs, beneath the lamp-light; the strong crust
Of friendly bread; and many-tasting food;
Rainbows; and the blue bitter smoke of wood;
And radiant raindrops couching in cool flowers;
And flowers themselves, that sway through sunny hours,
Dreaming of moths that drink them under the moon;
Then, the cool kindliness of sheets, that soon
Smooth away trouble; and the rough male kiss
Of blankets; grainy wood; live hair that is
Shining and free; blue-massing clouds; the keen
Unpassioned beauty of a great machine;
The benison of hot water; furs to touch;
The good smell of old clothes; and other such—
The comfortable smell of friendly fingers,
Hair's fragrance, and the musty reek that lingers
About dead leaves and last year's ferns ...

Rupert Brooke (1887–1915)

Returning, We Hear the Larks

Sombre the night is.
And though we have our lives, we know
What sinister threat lurks there.

Dragging these anguished limbs, we only know
This poison-blasted track opens on our camp—
On a little safe sleep.

But hark! joy—joy—strange joy.
Lo! heights of night ringing with unseen larks.
Music showering our upturned list'ning faces.

Death could drop from the dark
As easily as song—
But song only dropped,
Like a blind man's dreams on the sand
By dangerous tides,
Like a girl's dark hair for she dreams no ruin lies there,
Or her kisses where a serpent hides.

Isaac Rosenberg (1890–1918)

Circumstance

Down in the deep salt sea
  A mighty fish will make
Its own strong current, which
  The little ones must take;
Which they must follow still,
No matter for their will.

Here, in this human sea,
  Is Circumstance, that takes
Men where they're loth to go;
  It fits them false and makes
Machines of master souls,
And masters of dull fools.

W. H. Davies (1871–1940)

A voice that flowed along my dreams

FROM *THE PRELUDE* (1805), BOOK I

—Was it for this
That one, the fairest of all Rivers, loved
To blend his murmurs with my Nurse's song,
And from his alder shades and rocky falls,
And from his fords and shallows, sent a voice
That flowed along my dreams? For this, didst Thou,
O Derwent, travelling over the green Plains
Near my 'sweet Birthplace', didst thou, beauteous Stream,
Make ceaseless music through the night and day
Which with its steady cadence, tempering
Our human waywardness, composed my thoughts
To more than infant softness, giving me,
Among the fretful dwellings of mankind,
A knowledge, a dim earnest, of the calm
That Nature breathes among the hills and groves?
When, having left his Mountains, to the Towers
Of Cockermouth that beauteous River came,
Behind my Father's House he passed, close by,
Along the margin of our Terrace Walk.
He was a Playmate whom we dearly loved.

William Wordsworth (1770–1850)

So We'll Go No More A Roving

So, we'll go no more a roving
  So late into the night,
Though the heart be still as loving,
  And the moon be still as bright.

For the sword outwears its sheath,
  And the soul wears out the breast,
And the heart must pause to breathe,
  And Love itself have rest.

Though the night was made for loving,
  And the day returns too soon,
Yet we'll go no more a roving
  By the light of the moon.

Lord Byron (1788–1824)

The Tyger

Tyger Tyger, burning bright,
In the forests of the night;
What immortal hand or eye,
Could frame thy fearful symmetry?

In what distant deeps or skies.
Burnt the fire of thine eyes?
On what wings dare he aspire?
What the hand, dare seize the fire?

And what shoulder, & what art,
Could twist the sinews of thy heart?
And when thy heart began to beat,
What dread hand? & what dread feet?

What the hammer? what the chain,
In what furnace was thy brain?
What the anvil? what dread grasp,
Dare its deadly terrors clasp!

When the stars threw down their spears
And water'd heaven with their tears:
Did he smile his work to see?
Did he who made the Lamb make thee?

Tyger Tyger burning bright,
In the forests of the night:
What immortal hand or eye,
Dare frame thy fearful symmetry?

William Blake (1757–1827)

A Birthday

My heart is like a singing bird
Whose nest is in a watered shoot;
My heart is like an apple-tree
Whose boughs are bent with thickset fruit;
My heart is like a rainbow shell
That paddles in a halcyon sea;
My heart is gladder than all these
Because my love is come to me.

Raise me a dais of silk and down;
Hang it with vair and purple dyes;
Carve it in doves and pomegranates,
And peacocks with a hundred eyes;
Work it in gold and silver grapes,
In leaves and silver fleurs-de-lys;
Because the birthday of my life
Is come, my love is come to me.

Christina Rossetti (1830–1894)

The Golden Journey to Samarkand

FROM THE PLAY *HASSAN*

We are the Pilgrims, master; we shall go
　　Always a little further: it may be
Beyond that last blue mountain barred with snow,
　　Across that angry or that glimmering sea,

White on a throne or guarded in a cave
　　There lives a prophet who can understand
Why men were born: but surely we are brave,
　　Who take the Golden Road to Samarkand.

Sweet to ride forth at evening from the wells
　　When shadows pass gigantic on the sand,
And softly through the silence beat the bells
　　Along the Golden Road to Samarkand.

We travel not for trafficking alone;
　　By hotter winds our fiery hearts are fanned:
For lust of knowing what should not be known
　　We make the Golden Journey to Samarkand.

James Elroy Flecker (1884–1915)

The Homes of England

EXTRACT

The stately homes of England,
  How beautiful they stand!
Amidst their tall ancestral trees,
  O'er all the pleasant land!
The deer across their greensward bound
  Through shade and sunny gleam,
And the swan glides past them with the sound
  Of some rejoicing stream.

The merry homes of England!
  Around their hearths by night,
What gladsome looks of household love
  Meet in the ruddy light.
There woman's voice flows forth in song,
  Or childhood's tale is told;
Or lips move tunefully along
  Some glorious page of old.

The cottage homes of England!
  By thousands on her plains,
They are smiling o'er the silvery brooks,
  And round the hamlet-fanes.
Through glowing orchards forth they peep,
  Each from its nook of leaves;
And fearless there the lowly sleep,
  As the bird beneath their eaves.

Felicia Dorothea Hemans (1793–1835)

Farewell to the Farm

The coach is at the door at last;
The eager children, mounting fast
And kissing hands, in chorus sing:
Good-bye, good-bye, to everything!

To house and garden, field and lawn,
The meadow-gates we swang upon,
To pump and stable, tree and swing,
Good-bye, good-bye, to everything!

And fare you well for evermore,
O ladder at the hayloft door,
O hayloft where the cobwebs cling,
Good-bye, good-bye, to everything!

Crack goes the whip, and off we go;
The trees and houses smaller grow;
Last, round the woody turn we swing:
Good-bye, good-bye, to everything!

Robert Louis Stevenson (1850–1894)

Ozymandias

I met a traveller from an antique land,
Who said—'Two vast and trunkless legs of stone
Stand in the desert ... Near them, on the sand,
Half sunk a shattered visage lies, whose frown,
And wrinkled lip, and sneer of cold command,
Tell that its sculptor well those passions read
Which yet survive, stamped on these lifeless things,
The hand that mocked them, and the heart that fed;
And on the pedestal, these words appear:
My name is Ozymandias, King of Kings;
Look on my Works, ye Mighty, and despair!
Nothing beside remains. Round the decay
Of that colossal Wreck, boundless and bare
The lone and level sands stretch far away.'

Percy Bysshe Shelley (1792–1822)

SEPTEMBER

The Song of Earth

The smoke of my own breath

FROM *SONG OF MYSELF*, 1892

The smoke of my own breath,
Echoes, ripples, buzz'd whispers, love-root, silk-thread,
  crotch and vine,
My respiration and inspiration, the beating of my heart,
  the passing of blood and air through my lungs,
The sniff of green leaves and dry leaves, and of the shore
  and dark-color'd sea-rocks, and of hay in the barn,
                    * * * *
Stop this day and night with me and you shall possess
  the origin of all poems,
You shall possess the good of the earth and sun, (there
  are millions of suns left,)
You shall no longer take things at second or third hand,
  nor look through
  the eyes of the dead, nor feed on the spectres in books,
You shall not look through my eyes either, nor take
  things from me,
You shall listen to all sides and filter them from your self.

Walt Whitman (1819–1892)

When, in disgrace with fortune and men's eyes

SONNET XXIX

When, in disgrace with fortune and men's eyes,
I all alone beweep my outcast state,
And trouble deaf heaven with my bootless cries,
And look upon myself, and curse my fate,
Wishing me like to one more rich in hope,
Featured like him, like him with friends possessed,
Desiring this man's art and that man's scope,
With what I most enjoy contented least;
Yet in these thoughts myself almost despising,
Haply I think on thee, and then my state,
Like to the lark at break of day arising
From sullen earth, sings hymns at heaven's gate;
  For thy sweet love remembered such wealth brings
  That then I scorn to change my state with kings.

William Shakespeare (1564–1616)

Composed upon Westminster Bridge, September 3, 1802

Earth has not anything to show more fair:
Dull would he be of soul who could pass by
A sight so touching in its majesty:
This City now doth, like a garment, wear
The beauty of the morning; silent, bare,
Ships, towers, domes, theatres, and temples lie
Open unto the fields, and to the sky;
All bright and glittering in the smokeless air.
Never did sun more beautifully steep
In his first splendour, valley, rock, or hill;
Ne'er saw I, never felt, a calm so deep!
The river glideth at his own sweet will:
Dear God! the very houses seem asleep;
And all that mighty heart is lying still!

William Wordsworth (1770–1850)

Apples

Behold the apples' rounded worlds:
juice-green of July rain,
the black polestar of flowers, the rind
mapped with its crimson stain.

The russet, crab and cottage red
burn to the sun's hot brass,
then drop like sweat from every branch
and bubble in the grass.

They lie as wanton as they fall,
and where they fall and break,
the stallion clamps his crunching jaws,
the starling stabs his beak.

In each plump gourd the cidery bite
of boys' teeth tears the skin;
the waltzing wasp consumes his share,
the bent worm enters in.

I, with as easy hunger, take
entire my season's dole;
welcome the ripe, the sweet, the sour,
the hollow and the whole.

Laurie Lee (1914–1997)

A Leave-Taking

EXTRACT

Let us go hence, my songs; she will not hear.
Let us go hence together without fear;
Keep silence now, for singing-time is over,
And over all old things and all things dear.
She loves not you nor me as all we love her.
Yea, though we sang as angels in her ear,
    She would not hear.

Let us go hence and rest; she will not love.
She shall not hear us if we sing hereof,
Nor see love's ways, how sore they are and steep.
Come hence, let be, lie still; it is enough.
Love is a barren sea, bitter and deep;
And though she saw all heaven in flower above,
    She would not love.

Let us go hence, go hence; she will not see.
Sing all once more together; surely she,
She too, remembering days and words that were,
Will turn a little toward us, sighing; but we,
We are hence, we are gone, as though we had not been
    there.
Nay, and though all men seeing had pity on me,
    She would not see.

Algernon Charles Swinburne (1837–1909)

To Autumn

EXTRACT

Where are the songs of spring? Aye, Where are they?
    Think not of them, thou hast thy music too,—
While barrèd clouds bloom the soft-dying day,
    And touch the stubble-plains with rosy hue;
Then in a wailful choir the small gnats mourn
  Among the river sallows, borne aloft
        Or sinking as the light wind lives or dies;
And full-grown lambs loud bleat from hilly bourn;
    Hedge-crickets sing; and now with treble soft
    The red-breast whistles from a garden-croft;
        And gathering swallows twitter in the skies.

John Keats (1795–1821)

Robin Redbreast

Good-bye, good-bye to Summer!
　For Summer's nearly done;
The garden smiling faintly,
　Cool breezes in the sun;
Our Thrushes now are silent,
　Our Swallows flown away,—
But Robin's here, in coat of brown,
　With ruddy breast-knot gay.
Robin, Robin Redbreast,
　O Robin dear!
Robin singing sweetly
　In the falling of the year.

Bright yellow, red, and orange,
　The leaves come down in hosts;
The trees are Indian Princes,
　But soon they'll turn to Ghosts;
The scanty pears and apples
　Hang russet on the bough,
It's Autumn, Autumn, Autumn late,
　'Twill soon be Winter now.
Robin, Robin Redbreast,
　O Robin dear!
And welaway! my Robin,
　For pinching times are near.

The fireside for the Cricket,
  The wheatstack for the Mouse,
When trembling night-winds whistle
  And moan all round the house;
The frosty ways like iron,
  The branches plumed with snow,—
Alas! in Winter, dead and dark,
  Where can poor Robin go?
Robin, Robin Redbreast,
  O Robin dear,
And a crumb of bread for Robin,
  His little heart to cheer.

William Allingham (1824–1889)

The world is too much with us

The world is too much with us; late and soon,
Getting and spending we lay waste our powers;
Little we see in Nature that is ours;
We have given our hearts away, a sordid boon!
This Sea that bares her bosom to the moon,
The winds that will be howling at all hours,
And are up-gathered now like sleeping flowers,
For this, for everything, we are out of tune;
It moves us not.—Great God! I'd rather be
A Pagan suckled in a creed outworn;
So might I, standing on this pleasant lea,
Have glimpses that would make me less forlorn;
Have sight of Proteus rising from the sea;
Or hear old Triton blow his wreathèd horn.

William Wordsworth (1770–1850)

Fish say

FROM *HEAVEN*

Fish say, they have their Stream and Pond;
But is there anything Beyond?
This life cannot be All, they swear,
For how unpleasant, if it were!
One may not doubt that, somehow, Good
Shall come of Water and of Mud;
And, sure, the reverent eye must see
A Purpose in Liquidity.
We darkly know, by Faith we cry,
The future is not Wholly Dry.
Mud unto mud!—Death eddies near—
Not here the appointed End, not here!
But somewhere, beyond Space and Time
Is wetter water, slimier slime!
And there (they trust) there swimmeth One
Who swam ere rivers were begun,
Immense, of fishy form and mind,
Squamous, omnipotent, and kind;
And under that Almighty Fin,
The littlest fish may enter in.

Rupert Brooke (1887–1915)

Infant Sorrow

My mother groand! my father wept.
Into the dangerous world I leapt:
Helpless, naked, piping loud;
Like a fiend hid in a cloud.

Struggling in my fathers hands:
Striving against my swaddling bands:
Bound and weary I thought best
To sulk upon my mothers breast.

William Blake (1757–1827)

Morning Song

Love set you going like a fat gold watch.
The midwife slapped your footsoles, and your bald cry
Took its place among the elements.

Our voices echo, magnifying your arrival. New statue.
In a drafty museum, your nakedness
Shadows our safety. We stand round blankly as walls.

I'm no more your mother
Than the cloud that distills a mirror to reflect its own slow
Effacement at the wind's hand.

All night your moth-breath
Flickers among the flat pink roses. I wake to listen:
A far sea moves in my ear.

One cry, and I stumble from bed, cow-heavy and floral
In my Victorian nightgown.
Your mouth opens clean as a cat's. The window square

Whitens and swallows its dull stars. And now you try
Your handful of notes;
The clear vowels rise like balloons.

Sylvia Plath (1932–1963)

In words, like weeds, I'll wrap me o'er

FROM *IN MEMORIAM A.H.H.*

I sometimes hold it half a sin
  To put in words the grief I feel;
  For words, like Nature, half reveal
And half conceal the Soul within.

But, for the unquiet heart and brain,
  A use in measured language lies;
  The sad mechanic exercise,
Like dull narcotics, numbing pain.

In words, like weeds, I'll wrap me o'er,
  Like coarsest clothes against the cold;
  But that large grief which these enfold
Is given in outline and no more.

Alfred, Lord Tennyson (1809–1892)

The Sea

FROM *CHILDE HAROLD'S PILGRIMAGE*, CANTO IV

There is a pleasure in the pathless woods,
There is a rapture on the lonely shore,
There is society where none intrudes,
By the deep Sea, and music in its roar:
I love not Man the less, but Nature more,
From these our interviews, in which I steal
From all I may be, or have been before,
To mingle with the Universe, and feel
What I can ne'er express, yet cannot all conceal.

Lord Byron (1788–1824)

Listening

'Tis you that are the music, not your song.
The song is but a door which, opening wide,
Lets forth the pent-up melody inside,
Your spirit's harmony, which clear and strong
Sings but of you. Throughout your whole life long
Your songs, your thoughts, your doings, each divide
This perfect beauty; waves within a tide,
Or single notes amid a glorious throng.
The song of earth has many different chords;
Ocean has many moods and many tones
Yet always ocean. In the damp Spring woods
The painted trillium smiles, while crisp pine cones
Autumn alone can ripen. So is this
One music with a thousand cadences.

Amy Lowell (1874–1925)

Trees

The Oak is called the king of trees,
The Aspen quivers in the breeze,
The Poplar grows up straight and tall,
The Peach-tree spreads along the wall,
The Sycamore gives pleasant shade,
The Willow droops in watery glade,
The Fir-tree useful in timber gives,
The Beech amid the forest lives.

Sara Coleridge (1802–1852)

Moonlit Apples

At the top of the house the apples are laid in rows,
And the skylight lets the moonlight in, and those
Apples are deep-sea apples of green. There goes
   A cloud on the moon in the autumn night.

A mouse in the wainscot scratches, and scratches, and then
There is no sound at the top of the house of men
Or mice; and the cloud is blown, and the moon again
   Dapples the apples with deep-sea light.

They are lying in rows there, under the gloomy beams;
On the sagging floor; they gather the silver streams
Out of the moon, those moonlit apples of dreams,
   And quiet is the steep stair under.

In the corridors under there is nothing but sleep.
And stiller than ever on orchard boughs they keep
Tryst with the moon, and deep is the silence, deep
   On moon-washed apples of wonder.

John Drinkwater (1882–1937)

Meg Merrilies

Old Meg she was a Gipsy,
  And liv'd upon the Moors:
Her bed it was the brown heath turf,
  And her house was out of doors.

Her apples were swart blackberries,
  Her currants pods o' broom;
Her wine was dew of the wild white rose,
  Her book a churchyard tomb.

Her Brothers were the craggy hills,
  Her Sisters larchen trees—
Alone with her great family
  She liv'd as she did please.

No breakfast had she many a morn,
  No dinner many a noon,
And 'stead of supper she would stare
  Full hard against the Moon.

But every morn of woodbine fresh
  She made her garlanding,
And every night the dark glen Yew
  She wove, and she would sing.

And with her fingers old and brown
  She plaited Mats o' Rushes,
And gave them to the Cottagers
  She met among the Bushes.

Old Meg was brave as Margaret Queen
  And tall as Amazon:
An old red blanket cloak she wore;
  A chip hat had she on.
God rest her aged bones somewhere—
  She died full long agone!

John Keats (1795–1821)

Happy the man

FROM *HORACE, ODES*, BOOK III, XXIX

Happy the man, and happy he alone,
   He, who can call today his own:
   He who, secure within, can say,
Tomorrow do thy worst, for I have lived today.
   Be fair, or foul, or rain, or shine,
The joys I have possessed, in spite of fate are mine,
   Not Heaven itself upon the past has power,
But what has been, has been, and I have had my hour.

John Dryden (1631–1700)

The Owl

Downhill I came, hungry, and yet not starved;
Cold, yet had heat within me that was proof
Against the North wind; tired, yet so that rest
Had seemed the sweetest thing under a roof.

Then at the inn I had food, fire, and rest,
Knowing how hungry, cold, and tired was I.
All of the night was quite barred out except
An owl's cry, a most melancholy cry

Shaken out long and clear upon the hill,
No merry note, nor cause of merriment,
But one telling me plain what I escaped
And others could not, that night, as in I went.

And salted was my food, and my repose,
Salted and sobered, too, by the bird's voice
Speaking for all who lay under the stars,
Soldiers and poor, unable to rejoice.

Edward Thomas (1878–1917)

Where love once was

Where love once was, let there be no hate:
Though they that went as one by night and day
Go now alone,
Where love once was, let there be no hate.

The seeds we planted together
Came to rich harvest,
And our hearts are as bins brimming with the golden
  plenty:
Into our loneliness we carry granaries of old love ...

And though the time has come when we cannot sow our
  acres together,
And our souls need diverse fields,
And a tilling apart,
Let us go separate ways with a blessing each for each,
And gentle parting,
And let there be no hate,
Where love once was.

James Oppenheim (1882–1932)

A thing of beauty is a joy for ever

FROM *ENDYMION*, BOOK I

A thing of beauty is a joy for ever:
Its loveliness increases; it will never
Pass into nothingness; but still will keep
A bower quiet for us, and a sleep
Full of sweet dreams, and health, and quiet breathing.
Therefore, on every morrow, are we wreathing
A flowery band to bind us to the earth,
Spite of despondence, of the inhuman dearth
Of noble natures, of the gloomy days,
Of all the unhealthy and o'er-darkened ways
Made for our searching: yes, in spite of all,
Some shape of beauty moves away the pall
From our dark spirits. Such the sun, the moon,
Trees old, and young, sprouting a shady boon
For simple sheep; and such are daffodils
With the green world they live in; and clear rills
That for themselves a cooling covert make
'Gainst the hot season; the mid-forest brake,
Rich with a sprinkling of fair musk-rose blooms:
And such too is the grandeur of the dooms
We have imagined for the mighty dead;
All lovely tales that we have heard or read:
An endless fountain of immortal drink,
Pouring unto us from the heaven's brink.

John Keats (1795–1821)

Autumn

FROM *THE FAERIE QUEENE*

Then came the *Autumn* all in yellow clad,
As though he joyed in his plenteous store,
Laden with fruits that made him laugh, full glad
That he had banished hunger, which to-fore
Had by the belly oft him pinchèd sore:
Upon his head a wreath, that was enrold
With ears of corn of every sort, he bore:
And in his hand a sickle he did hold,
To reap the ripen'd fruits the which the earth had yold.

Edmund Spenser (1552–1599)

Block City

What are you able to build with your blocks?
Castles and palaces, temples and docks.
Rain may keep raining and others go roam,
But I can be happy and building at home.

Let the sofa be mountains, the carpet be sea,
There I'll establish a city for me:
A kirk and a mill and a palace beside,
And a harbor as well where my vessels may ride.

Great is the palace with pillar and wall,
A sort of a tower on the top of it all,
And steps coming down in an orderly way
To where my toy vessels lay safe in the bay.

This one is sailing and that one is moored:
Hark to the song of the sailors on board!
And see the steps of my palace, the kings
Coming and going with presents and things!

Now I have done with it, down let it go!
All in a moment the town is laid low.
Block upon block lying scattered and free,
What is there left of my town by the sea?

Yet as I saw it, I see it again,
The kirk and the palace, the ships and the men
And as long as I live and where'er I may be,
I'll always remember my town by the sea.

Robert Louis Stevenson (1850–1894)

The Road Not Taken

Two roads diverged in a yellow wood,
And sorry I could not travel both
And be one traveler, long I stood
And looked down one as far as I could
To where it bent in the undergrowth;

Then took the other, as just as fair,
And having perhaps the better claim,
Because it was grassy and wanted wear;
Though as for that, the passing there
Had worn them really about the same,

And both that morning equally lay
In leaves no step had trodden black.
Oh, I kept the first for another day!
Yet knowing how way leads on to way
I doubted if I should ever come back.

I shall be telling this with a sigh
Somewhere ages and ages hence:
Two roads diverged in a wood, and I—
I took the one less traveled by,
And that has made all the difference.

Robert Frost (1874–1963)

Too late for love

FROM *THE PRINCE'S PROGRESS*

'Too late for love, too late for joy,
　　Too late, too late!
You loitered on the road too long,
　　You trifled at the gate:
The enchanted dove upon her branch
　　Died without a mate;
The enchanted princess in her tower
　　Slept, died, behind the grate;
Her heart was starving all this while
　　You made it wait.'

Christina Rossetti (1830–1894)

Funeral Blues

Stop all the clocks, cut off the telephone,
Prevent the dog from barking with a juicy bone,
Silence the pianos and with muffled drum
Bring out the coffin, let the mourners come.

Let aeroplanes circle moaning overhead
Scribbling on the sky the message He is Dead,
Put crepe bows round the white necks of the public doves,
Let the traffic policemen wear black cotton gloves.

He was my North, my South, my East and West,
My working week and my Sunday rest,
My noon, my midnight, my talk, my song,
I thought that love would last forever: I was wrong.

The stars are not wanted now: put out every one;
Pack up the moon and dismantle the sun;
Pour away the ocean and sweep up the wood.
For nothing now can ever come to any good.

W. H. Auden (1907–1973)

An Irish Airman Foresees His Death

I know that I shall meet my fate
Somewhere among the clouds above;
Those that I fight I do not hate,
Those that I guard I do not love;
My country is Kiltartan Cross,
My countrymen Kiltartan's poor,
No likely end could bring them loss
Or leave them happier than before.
Nor law, nor duty bade me fight,
Nor public men, nor cheering crowds,
A lonely impulse of delight
Drove to this tumult in the clouds;
I balanced all, brought all to mind,
The years to come seemed waste of breath,
A waste of breath the years behind
In balance with this life, this death.

W. B. Yeats (1865–1939)

Let This Darkness Be a Bell Tower

FROM *SONNETS TO ORPHEUS* II, XXIX

Quiet friend who has come so far,
feel how your breathing makes more space around you.
Let this darkness be a bell tower
and you the bell. As you ring,

what batters you becomes your strength.
Move back and forth into the change.
What is it like, such intensity of pain?
If the drink is bitter, turn yourself to wine.

In this uncontainable night,
be the mystery at the crossroads of your senses,
the meaning discovered there.

And if the world has ceased to hear you,
say to the silent earth: I flow.
To the rushing water, speak: I am.

Rainer Maria Rilke (1875–1926)
Translated from the German by Joanna Macy (b. 1929)
and Anita Barrows (b. 1947)

Not Love Perhaps

This is not Love perhaps—Love that lays down
Its life, that many waters cannot quench, nor the floods
  drown—
But something written in lighter ink, said in a lower tone:
Something perhaps especially our own:
A need at times to be together and talk—
And then the finding we can walk
More firmly through dark narrow places
And meet more easily nightmare faces:
A need to reach out sometimes hand to hand—
And then find Earth less like an alien land:
A need for alliance to defeat
The whisperers at the corner of the street:
A need for inns on roads, islands in seas, halts for
  discoveries to be shared,
Maps checked and notes compared:
A need at times of each for each
Direct as the need of throat and tongue for speech.

Arthur Seymour John Tessimond (1902–1962)

In souls a sympathy with sounds

FROM *THE TASK*, BOOK VI

There is in souls a sympathy with sounds,
And as the mind is pitched the ear is pleased
With melting airs or martial, brisk or grave;
Some chord in unison with what we hear
Is touched within us, and the heart replies.
How soft the music of those village bells
Falling at intervals upon the ear
In cadence sweet, now dying all away,
Now pealing loud again, and louder still,
Clear and sonorous as the gale comes on.
With easy force it opens all the cells
Where memory slept. Wherever I have heard
A kindred melody, the scene recurs,
And with it all its pleasures and its pains.
Such comprehensive views the spirit takes,
That in a few short moments I retrace
(As in a map the voyager his course)
The windings of my way through many years.

William Cowper (1731–1800)

OCTOBER

Altitude of Loveliness

Delicious Autumn!

ADAPTED FROM A LETTER WRITTEN TO MISS LEWIS,
1ST OCTOBER 1841

Is not this a true autumn day?
Just the still melancholy that I love—
That makes life and nature harmonize.

The birds are consulting about their migrations,
The trees are putting on the hectic or the pallid hues of
　decay,
And begin to strew the ground,
That one's very footsteps may not disturb
The repose of earth and air,
While they give us a scent
That is a perfect anodyne to the restless spirit.

Delicious autumn!
My very soul is wedded to it.
And if I were a bird
I would fly about the earth
Seeking the successive autumns.

George Eliot (1819–1880)

Begin

Begin again to the summoning birds
to the sight of light at the window,
begin to the roar of morning traffic
all along Pembroke Road.
Every beginning is a promise
born in light and dying in dark
determination and exaltation of springtime
flowering the way to work.
Begin to the pageant of queuing girls
the arrogant loneliness of swans in the canal
bridges linking the past and future
old friends passing though with us still.
Begin to the loneliness that cannot end
since it perhaps is what makes us begin,
begin to wonder at unknown faces
at crying birds in the sudden rain
at branches stark in the willing sunlight
at seagulls foraging for bread
at couples sharing a sunny secret
alone together while making good.
Though we live in a world that dreams of ending
that always seems about to give in
something that will not acknowledge conclusion
insists that we forever begin.

Brendan Kennelly (1936–2021)

October

It is no joy to me to sit
   On dreamy summer eves,
When silently the timid moon
   Kisses the sleeping leaves,
And all things through the fair hushed earth
   Love, rest—but nothing grieves.
Better I like old Autumn
   With his hair tossed to and fro,
Firm striding o'er the stubble fields
When the equinoctials blow.

When shrinkingly the sun creeps up
   Through misty mornings cold,
And Robin on the orchard hedge
   Sings cheerily and bold,
While the heavily frosted plum
   Drops downward on the mould;—
And as he passes, Autumn
   Into earth's lap does throw
Brown apples gay in a game of play,
   As the equinoctials blow.

When the spent year its carol sinks
    Into a humble psalm,
Asks no more for the pleasure draught,
    But for the cup of balm,
And all its storms and sunshine bursts
    Controls to one brave calm,—
Then step by step walks Autumn,
    With steady eyes that show
Nor grief nor fear, to the death of the year,
    While the equinoctials blow.

Dinah Maria Craik (1826–1887)

For quiet, friend, the soldier fights

FROM ODE XVI, *TO POMPEIUS GROSPHUS*

In storms when clouds the moon do hide,
And no kind stars the pilot guide,
Show me at sea the boldest there
Who does not wish for quiet here.

For quiet, friend, the soldier fights,
Bears weary marches, sleepless nights,
For this feeds hard and lodges cold,
Which can't be bought with hills of gold.

Quintus Horatius Flaccus (Horace) (65–8 BC)
Translated from the Latin by Thomas Otway (1652–1685)

Still I Rise

You may write me down in history
With your bitter, twisted lies,
You may tread me in the very dirt
But still, like dust, I'll rise.

Does my sassiness upset you?
Why are you beset with gloom?
'Cause I walk like I've got oil wells
Pumping in my living room.

Just like moons and like suns,
With the certainty of tides,
Just like hopes springing high,
Still I'll rise.

Did you want to see me broken?
Bowed head and lowered eyes?
Shoulders falling down like teardrops.
Weakened by my soulful cries.

Does my haughtiness offend you?
Don't you take it awful hard
'Cause I laugh like I've got gold mines
Diggin' in my own back yard.

You may shoot me with your words,
You may cut me with your eyes,
You may kill me with your hatefulness,
But still, like air, I'll rise.

Does my sexiness upset you?
Does it come as a surprise
That I dance like I've got diamonds
At the meeting of my thighs?

Out of the huts of history's shame
I rise
Up from a past that's rooted in pain
I rise
I'm a black ocean, leaping and wide,
Welling and swelling I bear in the tide.

Leaving behind nights of terror and fear
I rise
Into a daybreak that's wondrously clear
I rise
Bringing the gifts that my ancestors gave,
I am the dream and the hope of the slave.
I rise
I rise
I rise.

Maya Angelou (1928–2014)

The Swan

Did you too see it, drifting, all night, on the black river?
Did you see it in the morning, rising into the silvery air,
an armful of white blossoms,
a perfect commotion of silk and linen as it leaned
into the bondage of its wings: a snowbank, a bank of lilies,
biting the air with its black beak?
Did you hear it, fluting and whistling
a shrill dark music, like the rain pelting the trees,
   like a waterfall
knifing down the black ledges?
And did you see it, finally, just under the clouds—
a white cross streaming across the sky, its feet
like black leaves, its wings like the stretching light
   of the river?
And did you feel it, in your heart, how it pertained to
   everything?
And have you too finally figured out what beauty is for?
And have you changed your life?

Mary Oliver (1935–2019)

The Wild Swans at Coole

The trees are in their autumn beauty,
The woodland paths are dry,
Under the October twilight the water
Mirrors a still sky;
Upon the brimming water among the stones
Are nine-and-fifty swans.

The nineteenth autumn has come upon me
Since I first made my count;
I saw, before I had well finished,
All suddenly mount
And scatter wheeling in great broken rings
Upon their clamorous wings.

I have looked upon those brilliant creatures,
And now my heart is sore.
All's changed since I, hearing at twilight,
The first time on this shore,
The bell-beat of their wings above my head,
Trod with a lighter tread.

Unwearied still, lover by lover,
They paddle in the cold
Companionable streams or climb the air;
Their hearts have not grown old;
Passion or conquest, wander where they will,
Attend upon them still.

But now they drift on the still water,
Mysterious, beautiful;
Among what rushes will they build,
By what lake's edge or pool
Delight men's eyes when I awake some day
To find they have flown away?

W. B. Yeats (1865–1939)

Tears, idle tears

FROM *THE PRINCESS*

Tears, idle tears, I know not what they mean,
Tears from the depth of some divine despair
Rise in the heart, and gather to the eyes,
In looking on the happy Autumn-fields,
And thinking of the days that are no more.

Fresh as the first beam glittering on a sail,
That brings our friends up from the underworld,
Sad as the last which reddens over one
That sinks with all we love below the verge;
So sad, so fresh, the days that are no more.

Ah, sad and strange as in dark summer dawns
The earliest pipe of half-awakened birds
To dying ears, when unto dying eyes
The casement slowly grows a glimmering square;
So sad, so strange, the days that are no more.

Dear as remembered kisses after death,
And sweet as those by hopeless fancy feigned
On lips that are for others; deep as love,
Deep as first love, and wild with all regret;
O Death in Life, the days that are no more.

Alfred, Lord Tennyson (1809–1892)

Speech To The Young: Speech To The Progress-Toward (Among them Nora and Henry III)

Say to them,
say to the down-keepers,
the sun-slappers,
the self-soilers,
the harmony-hushers,
'Even if you are not ready for day
it cannot always be night.'
You will be right.
For that is the hard home-run.

Live not for battles won.
Live not for the-end-of-the-song.
Live in the along.

Gwendolyn Brooks (1917–2000)

I Hear America Singing

I hear America singing, the varied carols I hear,
Those of mechanics, each one singing his as it should be
    blithe and strong,
The carpenter singing his as he measures his plank or beam,
The mason singing his as he makes ready for work, or
    leaves off work,
The boatman singing what belongs to him in his boat, the
    deck-hand singing on the steamboat deck,
The shoemaker singing as he sits on his bench, the hatter
    singing as he stands,
The wood-cutter's song, the ploughboy's on his way in the
    morning, or at noon intermission or at sundown,
The delicious singing of the mother, or of the young wife
    at work, or of the girl sewing or washing,
Each singing what belongs to him or her and to none
    else,
The day what belongs to the day—at night the party of
    young fellows, robust, friendly,
Singing with open mouths their strong melodious songs.

Walt Whitman (1819–1892)

Give me my scallop shell of quiet

FROM *THE PASSIONATE MAN'S PILGRIMAGE*

Give me my scallop shell of quiet,
My staff of faith to walk upon,
My scrip of joy, immortal diet,
My bottle of salvation,
My gown of glory, hope's true gage,
And thus I'll take my pilgrimage.

Sir Walter Ralegh (1554–1618)

Forlorn

I have lived and I have loved;
    I have waked and I have slept;
I have sung and I have danced;
    I have smiled and I have wept;
I have won and wasted treasure;
I have had my fill of pleasure;
And all these things were weariness,
And some of them were dreariness;—
And all these things, but two things,
    Were emptiness and pain:
And Love—it was the best of them,—
And Sleep—worth all the rest of them,
    Worth everything but Love to my spirit and my brain.
But still, my friend, O Slumber,
Till my days complete their number,
    For Love shall never, never return to me again!

Charles Mackay (1814–1889)

Ode to the West Wind

EXTRACT

O wild West Wind, thou breath of Autumn's being,
Thou, from whose unseen presence the leaves dead
Are driven, like ghosts from an enchanter fleeing,

Yellow, and black, and pale, and hectic red,
Pestilence-stricken multitudes: O thou,
Who chariotest to their dark wintry bed

The winged seeds, where they lie cold and low,
Each like a corpse within its grave, until
Thine azure sister of the Spring shall blow

Her clarion o'er the dreaming earth, and fill
(Driving sweet buds like flocks to feed in air)
With living hues and odours plain and hill:

Wild Spirit, which art moving everywhere;
Destroyer and preserver; hear, oh hear!

Percy Bysshe Shelley (1792–1822)

Song: The Owl

When cats run home and light is come,
  And dew is cold upon the ground,
And the far-off stream is dumb,
  And the whirring sail goes round,
  And the whirring sail goes round;
    Alone and warming his five wits,
    The white owl in the belfry sits.

When merry milkmaids click the latch,
  And rarely smells the new-mown hay,
And the cock hath sung beneath the thatch
  Twice or thrice his roundelay,
  Twice or thrice his roundelay;
    Alone and warming his five wits,
    The white owl in the belfry sits.

Alfred, Lord Tennyson (1809–1892)

The Buried Life

EXTRACT

Only—but this is rare—
When a belovèd hand is laid in ours,
When, jaded with the rush and glare
Of the interminable hours,
Our eyes can in another's eyes read clear,
When our world-deafen'd ear
Is by the tones of a loved voice caress'd—
A bolt is shot back somewhere in our breast,
And a lost pulse of feeling stirs again.
The eye sinks inward, and the heart lies plain,
And what we mean, we say, and what we would, we know.
A man becomes aware of his life's flow,
And hears its winding murmur, and he sees
The meadows where it glides, the sun, the breeze.

And there arrives a lull in the hot race
Wherein he doth for ever chase
The flying and elusive shadow, rest.
An air of coolness plays upon his face,
And an unwonted calm pervades his breast.
And then he thinks he knows
The hills where his life rose,
And the sea where it goes.

Matthew Arnold (1822–1888)

Outlook

Not to be conquered by these headlong days,
    But to stand free: to keep the mind at brood
    On life's deep meaning, nature's altitude
Of loveliness, and time's mysterious ways;
At every thought and deed to clear the haze
    Out of our eyes, considering only this,
    What man, what life, what love, what beauty is,
This is to live, and win the final praise.

Though strife, ill fortune, and harsh human need
    Beat down the soul, at moments blind and dumb
    With agony; yet patience—there shall come
    Many great voices from life's outer sea,
Hours of strange triumph, and when few men heed,
    Murmurs and glimpses of eternity.

Archibald Lampman (1861–1899)

Casabianca

The boy stood on the burning deck
  Whence all but he had fled;
The flame that lit the battle's wreck
  Shone round him o'er the dead.

Yet beautiful and bright he stood,
  As born to rule the storm—
A creature of heroic blood,
  A proud, though child-like form.

The flames rolled on—he would not go
  Without his father's word;
That father, faint in death below,
  His voice no longer heard.

He called aloud—'Say, father, say
  If yet my task is done?'
He knew not that the chieftain lay
  Unconscious of his son.

'Speak, father!' once again he cried,
  'If I may yet be gone!
And'—but the booming shots replied,
  And fast the flames rolled on.

Upon his brow he felt their breath,
  And in his waving hair,
And looked from that lone post of death
  In still yet brave despair;

And shouted but once more aloud,
  'My father! must I stay?'
While o'er him fast, through sail and shroud,
  The wreathing fires made way.

They wrapt the ship in splendour wild,
  They caught the flag on high,
And streamed above the gallant child,
  Like banners in the sky.

There came a burst of thunder-sound—
  The boy—oh! where was he?
Ask of the winds that far around
  With fragments strewed the sea!—

With mast, and helm, and pennon fair,
  That well had borne their part—
But the noblest thing which perished there
  Was that young faithful heart.

Felicia Dorothea Hemans (1793–1835)

Prayer

Some days, although we cannot pray, a prayer
utters itself. So, a woman will lift
her head from the sieve of her hands and stare
at the minims sung by a tree, a sudden gift.

Some nights, although we are faithless, the truth
enters our hearts, that small familiar pain;
then a man will stand stock-still, hearing his youth
in the distant Latin chanting of a train.

Pray for us now. Grade 1 piano scales
console the lodger looking out across
a Midlands town. Then dusk, and someone calls
a child's name as though they named their loss.

Darkness outside. Inside, the radio's prayer—
Rockall. Malin. Dogger. Finisterre.

Carol Ann Duffy (b.1955)

Evening Solace

The human heart has hidden treasures,
In secret kept, in silence sealed;—
The thoughts, the hopes, the dreams, the pleasures,
Whose charms were broken if revealed.
And days may pass in gay confusion,
And nights in rosy riot fly,
While, lost in Fame's or Wealth's illusion,
The memory of the Past may die.

But, there are hours of lonely musing,
Such as in evening silence come,
When, soft as birds their pinions closing,
The heart's best feelings gather home.
Then in our souls there seems to languish
A tender grief that is not woe;
And thoughts that once wrung groans of anguish,
Now cause but some mild tears to flow.

And feelings, once as strong as passions,
Float softly back—a faded dream;
Our own sharp griefs and wild sensations,
The tale of others' sufferings seem.
Oh! when the heart is freshly bleeding,
How longs it for that time to be,
When, through the mist of years receding,
Its woes but live in reverie!

And it can dwell on moonlight glimmer,
On evening shade and loneliness;
And, while the sky grows dim and dimmer,
Feel no untold and strange distress—
Only a deeper impulse given
By lonely hour and darkened room,
To solemn thoughts that soar to heaven,
Seeking a life and world to come.

Charlotte Brontë (1816–1855)

O Radiant Dark

EXTRACT OF A SONG FROM *THE SPANISH GYPSY*

Dark the night, with breath all flowers,
And tender broken voice that fills
With ravishment the listening hours:
Whisperings, wooings,
Liquid ripples, and soft ring-dove cooings
In low-toned rhythm that love's aching stills.
Dark the night,
Yet is she bright,
For in her dark she brings the mystic star,
Trembling yet strong as is the voice of love,
From some unknown afar.
O radiant Dark! O darkly-fostered ray!
Thou hast a joy too deep for shallow Day.

George Eliot (1819–1880)

The Shut-Eye Train

EXTRACT

Over hill and over plain
Soon will speed the Shut-Eye train!
  Through the blue where bloom the stars
  And the Mother Moon looks down
    We'll away
    To land of Fay—
  Oh, the sights that we shall see there!
  Come, my little one, with me there—
'Tis a goodly train of cars—
All aboard for Shut-Eye Town!

Heavy are your eyes, my sweet,
Weary are your little feet—
  Nestle closer up to me
  In your pretty cap and gown;
    Don't detain
    The Shut-Eye train!
  'Ting-a-ling!' the bell it goeth,
  'Toot-toot!' the whistle bloweth
Oh, the sights that we shall see!
All aboard for Shut-Eye Town!

Eugene Field (1850–1895)

Night Mail

This is the night mail crossing the border,
Bringing the cheque and the postal order,
Letters for the rich, letters for the poor,
The shop at the corner and the girl next door.
Pulling up Beattock, a steady climb—
The gradient's against her, but she's on time.

Past cotton-grass and moorland boulder
Shovelling white steam over her shoulder,
Snorting noisily as she passes
Silent miles of wind-bent grasses;
Birds turn their heads as she approaches,
Stare from bushes at her blank-faced coaches;
Sheepdogs cannot turn her course
They slumber on with paws across.
In the farm she passes no one wakes,
But a jug in a bedroom gently shakes.

Dawn freshens, the climb is done.
Down towards Glasgow she descends
Towards the steam tugs, yelping down the glade of cranes
Towards the fields of apparatus, the furnaces
Set on the dark plain like gigantic chessmen.
All Scotland waits for her;
In dark glens, beside the pale-green lochs
Men long for news.

Letters of thanks, letters from banks,
Letters of joy from girl and boy,
Receipted bills and invitations
To inspect new stock or to visit relations,

And applications for situations,
And timid lovers' declarations,
And gossip, gossip from all the nations;
News circumstantial, news financial,
Letters with holiday snaps to enlarge in
Letters with faces scrawled on the margin.
Letters from uncles, cousins, and aunts,
Letters to Scotland from the South of France,
Letters of condolence to Highlands and Lowlands,
Notes from overseas to the Hebrides;
Written on paper of every hue
The pink, the violet, the white and the blue
The chatty, the catty, the boring, the adoring,
The cold and official and the heart's outpouring,
Clever, stupid, short and long,
The typed and the printed and the spelt all wrong.

Thousands are still asleep
Dreaming of terrifying monsters
Or a friendly tea beside the band in Cranston's or
    Crawford's;
Asleep in working Glasgow, asleep in well-set
    Edinburgh,
Asleep in granite Aberdeen.
They continue their dreams
But shall wake soon and hope for letters,
And none will hear the postman's knock
Without a quickening of the heart
For who can bear to feel himself forgotten?

W. H. Auden (1907–1973)

The Sound Collector

A stranger called this morning
Dressed all in black and grey
Put every sound into a bag
And carried them away

The whistling of the kettle
The turning of the lock
The purring of the kitten
The ticking of the clock

The popping of the toaster
The crunching of the flakes
When you spread the marmalade
The scraping noise it makes

The hissing of the frying-pan
The ticking of the grill
The bubbling of the bathtub
As it starts to fill

The drumming of the raindrops
On the window-pane
When you do the washing-up
The gurgle of the drain

The crying of the baby
The squeaking of the chair
The swishing of the curtain
The creaking of the stair

A stranger called this morning
He didn't leave his name
Left us only silence
Life will never be the same

Roger McGough (b.1937)

Remember

Remember me when I am gone away,
   Gone far away into the silent land;
   When you can no more hold me by the hand,
Nor I half turn to go yet turning stay.
Remember me when no more day by day
   You tell me of our future that you planned:
   Only remember me; you understand
It will be late to counsel then or pray.
Yet if you should forget me for a while
   And afterwards remember, do not grieve:
   For if the darkness and corruption leave
   A vestige of the thoughts that once I had,
Better by far you should forget and smile
   Than that you should remember and be sad.

Christina Rossetti (1830–1894)

My true love hath my heart

My true love hath my heart and I have his,
By just exchange one for the other given.
I hold his dear, and mine he cannot miss:
There never was a bargain better driven.
His heart in me keeps me and him in one;
My heart in him his thoughts and senses guides;
He loves my heart, for once it was his own;
I cherish his, because in me it bides.
His heart his wound receivèd from my sight;
My heart was wounded with his wounded heart;
For as from me on him his hurt did light,
So still, methought, in me his hurt did smart;
   Both equal hurt, in this change sought our bliss:
   My true love hath my heart and I have his.

Sir Philip Sidney (1554–1586)

He Wishes for the Cloths of Heaven

Had I the heavens' embroidered cloths,
Enwrought with golden and silver light,
The blue and the dim and the dark cloths
Of night and light and the half light,
I would spread the cloths under your feet:
But I, being poor, have only my dreams;
I have spread my dreams under your feet;
Tread softly because you tread on my dreams.

W. B. Yeats (1865–1939)

Even Such is Time

Even such is Time, that takes in trust
Our youth, our joys, our all we have,
And pays us but with earth and dust;
Who in the dark and silent grave,
When we have wander'd all our ways,
Shuts up the story of our days;
But from this earth, this grave, this dust,
My God shall raise me up, I trust.

Sir Walter Ralegh (1554–1618)

The Old Man's Comforts, and How he Gained Them

You are old, Father William, the young man cried,
  The few locks that are left you are grey;
You are hale, Father William, a hearty old man,
  Now tell me the reason, I pray.

In the days of my youth, Father William replied,
  I remember'd that youth would fly fast,
And abused not my health and my vigour at first
  That I never might need them at last.

You are old, Father William, the young man cried,
  And pleasures with youth pass away,
And yet you lament not the days that are gone,
  Now tell me the reason, I pray.

In the days of my youth, Father William replied,
    I remember'd that youth could not last;
I thought of the future whatever I did,
    That I never might grieve for the past.

You are old, Father William, the young man cried,
    And life must be hastening away;
You are chearful, and love to converse upon death!
    Now tell me the reason, I pray.

I am chearful, young man, Father William replied,
    Let the cause thy attention engage;
In the days of my youth I remember'd my God!
    And He hath not forgotten my age.

Robert Southey (1774–1843)

'You are old, Father William'

'You are old, Father William,' the young man said,
  'And your hair has become very white;
And yet you incessantly stand on your head—
  Do you think, at your age, it is right?'

'In my youth,' Father William replied to his son,
  'I feared it might injure the brain;
But, now that I'm perfectly sure I have none,
  Why, I do it again and again.'

'You are old,' said the youth, 'as I mentioned before,
  And have grown most uncommonly fat;
Yet you turned a back-somersault in at the door—
  Pray, what is the reason for that?'

'In my youth,' said the sage, as he shook his grey locks,
  'I kept all my limbs very supple
By the use of this ointment—one shilling a box—
  Allow me to sell you a couple?'

'You are old,' said the youth, 'and your jaws are too weak
  For anything tougher than suet;
Yet you finished the goose, with the bones and the beak—
  Pray, how did you manage to do it?'

'In my youth,' said his father, 'I took to the law,
    And argued each case with my wife;
And the muscular strength, which it gave to my jaw,
    Has lasted the rest of my life.'

'You are old,' said the youth, 'one would hardly suppose
    That your eye was as steady as ever;
Yet you balanced an eel on the end of your nose—
    What made you so awfully clever?'

'I have answered three questions, and that is enough,'
    Said his father. 'Don't give yourself airs!
Do you think I can listen all day to such stuff?
    Be off, or I'll kick you downstairs.'

Lewis Carroll (1832–1898)

Fear no more the heat o' the sun

SONG FROM *CYMBELINE*, ACT IV, SCENE II

Fear no more the heat o' the sun,
　　Nor the furious winter's rages;
Thou thy worldly task hast done,
　　Home art gone, and ta'en thy wages:
Golden lads and girls all must,
As chimney-sweepers, come to dust.

Fear no more the frown o' the great;
　　Thou art past the tyrant's stroke;
Care no more to clothe and eat;
　　To thee the reed is as the oak:
The sceptre, learning, physic, must
All follow this, and come to dust.

Fear no more the lightning flash,
　　Nor the all-dreaded thunder-stone;
Fear not slander, censure rash;
　　Thou hast finish'd joy and moan:
All lovers young, all lovers must
Consign to thee, and come to dust.

William Shakespeare (1564–1616)

Haunted Houses

EXTRACT

All houses wherein men have lived and died
   Are haunted houses. Through the open doors
The harmless phantoms on their errands glide,
   With feet that make no sound upon the floors.

We meet them at the door-way, on the stair,
   Along the passages they come and go,
Impalpable impressions on the air,
   A sense of something moving to and fro.

There are more guests at table than the hosts
   Invited; the illuminated hall
Is thronged with quiet, inoffensive ghosts,
   As silent as the pictures on the wall.

The stranger at my fireside cannot see
   The forms I see, nor hear the sounds I hear;
He but perceives what is; while unto me
   All that has been is visible and clear.

Henry Wadsworth Longfellow (1807–1882)

NOVEMBER

Seek the Quiet Hill

Jabberwocky

'Twas brillig, and the slithy toves
   Did gyre and gimble in the wabe:
All mimsy were the borogoves,
   And the mome raths outgrabe.

'Beware the Jabberwock, my son!
   The jaws that bite, the claws that catch!
Beware the Jubjub bird, and shun
   The frumious Bandersnatch!'

He took his vorpal sword in hand;
   Long time the manxome foe he sought—
So rested he by the Tumtum tree
   And stood awhile in thought.

And, as in uffish thought he stood,
   The Jabberwock, with eyes of flame,
Came whiffling through the tulgey wood,
   And burbled as it came!

One, two! One, two! And through and through
   The vorpal blade went snicker-snack!
He left it dead, and with its head
   He went galumphing back.

'And hast thou slain the Jabberwock?
   Come to my arms, my beamish boy!
O frabjous day! Callooh! Callay!'
   He chortled in his joy.

'Twas brillig, and the slithy toves
   Did gyre and gimble in the wabe:
All mimsy were the borogoves,
   And the mome raths outgrabe.

Lewis Carroll (1832–1898)

Lullaby of an Infant Chief

Air: 'ladul gu lo'*

O, hush thee, my babie, thy sire was a knight,
Thy mother a lady, both lovely and bright;
The woods and the glens, from the towers which we see,
They all are belonging, dear babie, to thee.
  O ho ro, i ri ri, cadul gu lo,
  O ho ro, i ri ri, cadul gu lo.

O, fear not the bugle, though loudly it blows,
It calls but the warders that guard thy repose;
Their bows would be bended, their blades would be red,
Ere the step of a foeman drew near to thy bed.
  O ho ro, i ri ri, cadul gu lo,
  O ho ro, i ri ri, cadul gu lo.

O, hush thee, my babie, the time soon will come
When thy sleep shall be broken by trumpet and drum;
Then hush thee, my darling, take rest while you may,
For strife comes with manhood, and waking with day.
  O ho ro, i ri ri, cadul gu lo,
  O ho ro, i ri ri, cadul gu lo.

*'sleep on till day'

Sir Walter Scott (1771–1832)

Witches' Song

FROM *THE MASQUE OF QUEENS*

The Owl is abroad, the Bat, and the Toad,
  And so is the Cat-a-mountain,
The Ant, and the Mole sit both in a hole,
  And Frog peeps out o' the Fountain;
The Dogs, they do bay, and the Timbrels play,
  The Spindle is now a-turning;
The Moon it is red, and the Stars are fled,
  But all the Sky is a-burning.

Ben Jonson (1572–1637)

Double, double toil and trouble

FROM *MACBETH*, ACT IV, SCENE I

Double, double toil and trouble;
Fire burn, and cauldron bubble.

Fillet of a fenny snake,
In the cauldron boil and bake;
Eye of newt and toe of frog,
Wool of bat and tongue of dog,
Adder's fork and blind-worm's sting,
Lizard's leg and owlet's wing,
For a charm of powerful trouble,
Like a hell-broth boil and bubble.

Double, double toil and trouble;
Fire burn and cauldron bubble.

William Shakespeare (1564–1616)

The Burning of the Leaves

EXTRACT

Now is the time for the burning of the leaves.
They go to the fire; the nostril pricks with smoke
Wandering slowly into a weeping mist.
Brittle and blotched, ragged and rotten sheaves!
A flame seizes the smouldering ruin and bites
On stubborn stalks that crackle as they resist.

The last hollyhock's fallen tower is dust;
All the spices of June are a bitter reek,
All the extravagant riches spent and mean.
All burns! The reddest rose is a ghost;
Sparks whirl up, to expire in the mist: the wild
Fingers of fire are making corruption clean.

Now is the time for stripping the spirit bare,
Time for the burning of days ended and done,
Idle solace of things that have gone before:
Rootless hope and fruitless desire are there;
Let them go to the fire, with never a look behind.
The world that was ours is a world that is ours no more.

They will come again, the leaf and the flower, to arise
From squalor of rottenness into the old splendour,
And magical scents to a wondering memory bring;
The same glory, to shine upon different eyes.
Earth cares for her own ruins, naught for ours.
Nothing is certain, only the certain spring.

Laurence Binyon (1869–1943)

Up-Hill

Does the road wind up-hill all the way?
  Yes, to the very end.
Will the day's journey take the whole long day?
  From morn to night, my friend.

But is there for the night a resting-place?
  A roof for when the slow dark hours begin.
May not the darkness hide it from my face?
  You cannot miss that inn.

Shall I meet other wayfarers at night?
  Those who have gone before.
Then must I knock, or call when just in sight?
  They will not keep you standing at that door.

Shall I find comfort, travel-sore and weak?
  Of labour you shall find the sum.
Will there be beds for me and all who seek?
  Yea, beds for all who come.

Christina Rossetti (1830–1894)

Severed Selves

Two separate divided silences,
   Which, brought together, would find loving voice;
   Two glances which together would rejoice
In love, now lost like stars beyond dark trees;
Two hands apart whose touch alone gives ease;
   Two bosoms which, heart-shrined with mutual flame,
   Would, meeting in one clasp, be made the same;
Two souls, the shores wave-mocked of sundering seas:—

Such are we now. Ah! may our hope forecast
   Indeed one hour again, when on this stream
   Of darkened love once more the light shall gleam?—
An hour how slow to come, how quickly past,—
Which blooms and fades, and only leaves at last,
   Faint as shed flowers, the attenuated dream.

Dante Gabriel Rossetti (1828–1882)

After the Winter

Some day, when trees have shed their leaves
    And against the morning's white
The shivering birds beneath the eaves
    Have sheltered for the night,
We'll turn our faces southward, love,
    Toward the summer isle
Where bamboos spire the shafted grove
    And wide-mouthed orchids smile.

And we will seek the quiet hill
    Where towers the cotton tree,
And leaps the laughing crystal rill,
    And works the droning bee.
And we will build a cottage there
    Beside an open glade,
With black-ribbed blue-bells blowing near,
    And ferns that never fade.

Claude McKay (1889–1948)

The Roads Also

The roads also have their wistful rest,
When the weather-cocks perch still and roost,
And the looks of men turn kind to clocks
And the trams go empty to their drome.
    The streets also dream their dream.

The old houses muse of the old days
And their fond trees leaning on them doze.
On their steps chatter and clatter stops
For the cries of other times hold men
    And they hear the unknown moan.

They remember alien ardours and far futures
And the smiles not seen in happy features.
Their begetters call them from the gutters;
In the gardens unborn child-souls wail,
    And the dead scribble on walls.

Though their own child cry for them in tears,
Women weep but hear no sound upstairs.
They believe in love they had not lived
And passion past the reach of stairs
    To the world's towers or stars.

Wilfred Owen (1893–1918)

Everyone Sang

Everyone suddenly burst out singing;
And I was filled with such delight
As prisoned birds must find in freedom,
Winging wildly across the white
Orchards and dark-green fields; on—on—and out of
   sight.

Everyone's voice was suddenly lifted;
And beauty came like the setting sun:
My heart was shaken with tears; and horror
Drifted away ... O, but Everyone
Was a bird; and the song was wordless; the singing will
   never be done.

Siegfried Sassoon (1886–1967)

They shall not grow old

FROM *FOR THE FALLEN*

They went with songs to the battle, they were young,
Straight of limb, true of eye, steady and aglow.
They were staunch to the end against odds uncounted;
They fell with their faces to the foe.

They shall grow not old, as we that are left grow old:
Age shall not weary them, nor the years condemn.
At the going down of the sun and in the morning
We will remember them.

They mingle not with their laughing comrades again;
They sit no more at familiar tables of home;
They have no lot in our labour of the day-time;
They sleep beyond England's foam.

Laurence Binyon (1869–1943)

To a Poet a Thousand Years Hence

I who am dead a thousand years,
   And wrote this sweet archaic song,
Send you my words for messengers
   The way I shall not pass along.

I care not if you bridge the seas,
   Or ride secure the cruel sky,
Or build consummate palaces
   Of metal or of masonry.

But have you wine and music still,
   And statues and a bright-eyed love,
And foolish thoughts of good and ill,
   And prayers to them who sit above?

How shall we conquer? Like a wind
   That falls at eve our fancies blow,
And old Moeonides the blind
   Said it three thousand years ago.

O friend unseen, unborn, unknown,
   Student of our sweet English tongue,
Read out my words at night, alone:
   I was a poet, I was young.

Since I can never see your face,
   And never shake you by the hand,
I send my soul through time and space
   To greet you. You will understand.

James Elroy Flecker (1884–1915)

Break, break, break

Break, break, break,
  On thy cold gray stones, O Sea!
And I would that my tongue could utter
  The thoughts that arise in me.

O, well for the fisherman's boy,
  That he shouts with his sister at play!
O, well for the sailor lad,
  That he sings in his boat on the bay!

And the stately ships go on
  To their haven under the hill;
But O for the touch of a vanish'd hand,
  And the sound of a voice that is still!

Break, break, break
  At the foot of thy crags, O Sea!
But the tender grace of a day that is dead
  Will never come back to me.

Alfred, Lord Tennyson (1809–1892)

Sea-Fever

I must go down to the seas again, to the lonely sea and
the sky,
And all I ask is a tall ship and a star to steer her by,
And the wheel's kick and the wind's song and the white
sail's shaking,
And a gray mist on the sea's face, and a gray dawn
breaking.

I must go down to the seas again, for the call of the
running tide
Is a wild call and a clear call that may not be denied;
And all I ask is a windy day with the white clouds flying,
And the flung spray and the blown spume, and the sea
gulls crying.

I must go down to the seas again, to the vagrant gypsy
life,
To the gull's way and the whale's way, where the wind's
like a whetted knife;
And all I ask is a merry yarn from a laughing fellow
rover,
And quiet sleep and a sweet dream when the long trick's
over.

John Masefield (1878–1967)

Mother to Son

Well, son, I'll tell you:
Life for me ain't been no crystal stair.
It's had tacks in it,
And splinters,
And boards torn up,
And places with no carpet on the floor—
Bare.
But all the time
I'se been a-climbin' on,
And reachin' landin's,
And turnin' corners,
And sometimes goin' in the dark
Where there ain't been no light.
So boy, don't you turn back.
Don't you set down on the steps
'Cause you finds it's kinder hard.
Don't you fall now—
For I'se still goin', honey,
I'se still climbin',
And life for me ain't been no crystal stair.

Langston Hughes (1901–1967)

Escape at Bedtime

The lights from the parlour and kitchen shone out
　　Through the blinds and the windows and bars;
And high over head and all moving about,
　　There were thousands of millions of stars.
There ne'er were such thousands of leaves on a tree,
　　Nor of people in church or the Park,
As the crowds of the stars looked down upon me,
　　And that glittered and winked in the dark.

The Dog, and the Plough, and the Hunter, and all,
　　And the star of the sailor, and Mars,
These shone in the sky, and the pail by the wall
　　Would be half full of water and stars.
They saw me at last, and they chased me with cries,
　　And they soon had me packed into bed;
But the glory kept shining and bright in my eyes,
　　And the stars going round in my head.

Robert Louis Stevenson (1850–1894)

The Star

Twinkle, twinkle, little star,
How I wonder what you are!
Up above the world so high,
Like a diamond in the sky.

When the blazing sun is gone,
When he nothing shines upon,
Then you show your little light,
Twinkle, twinkle, all the night.

Then the traveller in the dark
Thanks you for your tiny spark,
How could he see where to go,
If you did not twinkle so.

In the dark blue sky you keep,
Often through my curtains peep
For you never shut your eye,
Till the sun is in the sky.

As your bright and tiny spark
Lights the traveller in the dark,
Though I know not what you are,
Twinkle, twinkle, little star.

Jane Taylor (1783–1824)

To My Brothers

Small, busy flames play through the fresh laid coals,
  And their faint cracklings o'er our silence creep
  Like whispers of the household gods that keep
A gentle empire o'er fraternal souls.
And while, for rhymes, I search around the poles,
  Your eyes are fix'd, as in poetic sleep,
  Upon the lore so voluble and deep,
That aye at fall of night our care condoles.
This is your birth-day Tom, and I rejoice
  That thus it passes smoothly, quietly.
Many such eves of gently whisp'ring noise
  May we together pass, and calmly try
What are this world's true joys,—ere the great voice,
  From its fair face, shall bid our spirits fly.

November 18, 1816

John Keats (1795–1821)

Above the Dock

Above the quiet dock in mid night,
Tangled in the tall mast's corded height,
Hangs the moon. What seemed so far away
Is but a child's balloon, forgotten after play.

T. E. Hulme (1883–1917)

On the Ning Nang Nong

On the Ning Nang Nong
Where the Cows go Bong!
And the Monkeys all say Boo!
There's a Nong Nang Ning
Where the trees go Ping!
And the tea pots Jibber Jabber Joo.
On the Nong Ning Nang
All the mice go Clang!
And you just can't catch 'em when they do!
So it's Ning Nang Nong!
Cows go Bong!
Nong Nang Ning!
Trees go Ping!
Nong Ning Nang!
The mice go Clang!
What a noisy place to belong,
Is the Ning Nang
  Ning Nang Nong! !

Spike Milligan (1918–2002)

The Cow

The friendly cow all red and white,
   I love with all my heart:
She gives me cream with all her might,
   To eat with apple-tart.

She wanders lowing here and there,
   And yet she cannot stray,
All in the pleasant open air,
   The pleasant light of day;

And blown by all the winds that pass
   And wet with all the showers,
She walks among the meadow grass
   And eats the meadow flowers.

Robert Louis Stevenson (1850–1894)

As You Go Through Life

Don't look for the flaws as you go through life;
   And even when you find them,
It is wise and kind to be somewhat blind
   And look for the virtue behind them;
For the cloudiest night has a hint of light
   Somewhere in its shadows hiding;
It is better by far to hunt for a star,
   Than the spots on the sun abiding.

The current of life runs ever away
   To the bosom of God's great ocean.
Don't set your force 'gainst the river's course,
   And think to alter its motion.
Don't waste a curse on the universe,
   Remember it lived before you;
Don't butt at the storm with your puny form,
   But bend and let it go o'er you.

The world will never adjust itself
   To suit your whims to the letter;
Some things must go wrong your whole life long,
   And the sooner you know it the better.
It is folly to fight with the Infinite,
   And go under at last in the wrestle.
The wiser man shapes into God's plan,
   As water shapes into a vessel.

Ella Wheeler Wilcox (1850–1919)

Often rebuked, yet always back returning

Often rebuked, yet always back returning
  To those first feelings that were born with me,
And leaving busy chase of wealth and learning
  For idle dreams of things which cannot be:

To-day, I will seek not the shadowy region;
  Its unsustaining vastness waxes drear;
And visions rising, legion after legion,
  Bring the unreal world too strangely near.

I'll walk, but not in old heroic traces,
  And not in paths of high morality,
And not among the half-distinguished faces,
  The clouded forms of long-past history.

I'll walk where my own nature would be leading:
  It vexes me to choose another guide:
Where the grey flocks in ferny glens are feeding,
  Where the wild wind blows on the mountain side.

What have those lonely mountains worth revealing?
  More glory and more grief than I can tell:
The earth that wakes one human heart to feeling
  Can centre both the worlds of Heaven and Hell.

Emily Brontë (1818–1848)

Address to a Child During a Boisterous Winter Evening

EXTRACT

What way does the wind come? What way does he go?
He rides over the water, and over the snow,
Through wood, and through vale; and o'er rocky height,
Which the goat cannot climb, takes his sounding flight;
He tosses about in every bare tree,
As, if you look up, you plainly may see;
But how he will come, and whither he goes,
There's never a scholar in England knows.

Dorothy Wordsworth (1771–1855)

Remember

Remember the sky that you were born under,
know each of the star's stories.
Remember the moon, know who she is.
Remember the sun's birth at dawn, that is the
strongest point of time. Remember sundown
and the giving away to night.
Remember your birth, how your mother struggled
to give you form and breath. You are evidence of
her life, and her mother's, and hers.
Remember your father. He is your life, also.
Remember the earth whose skin you are:
red earth, black earth, yellow earth, white earth
brown earth, we are earth.
Remember the plants, trees, animal life who all have their
tribes, their families, their histories, too. Talk to them,
listen to them. They are alive poems.
Remember the wind. Remember her voice. She knows the
origin of this universe.
Remember you are all people and all people
are you.
Remember you are this universe and this
universe is you.
Remember all is in motion, is growing, is you.
Remember language comes from this.
Remember the dance language is, that life is.
Remember.

Joy Harjo (b.1951)

To see a world in a grain of sand

FROM *AUGURIES OF INNOCENCE*

To see a World in a Grain of Sand
And a Heaven in a Wild Flower
Hold Infinity in the palm of your hand
And Eternity in an hour

William Blake (1757–1827)

To the Rain

Mother rain, manifold, measureless,
falling on fallow, on field and forest,
on house-roof, low hovel, high tower,
downwelling waters all-washing, wider
than cities, softer than sisterhood, vaster
than countrysides, calming, recalling:
return to us, teaching our troubled
souls in your ceaseless descent
to fall, to be fellow, to feel to the root,
to sink in, to heal, to sweeten the sea.

Ursula K. Le Guin (1929–2018)

Hope

Hope is the thing with feathers
That perches in the soul,
And sings the tune without the words,
And never stops at all,

And sweetest in the gale is heard;
And sore must be the storm
That could abash the little bird,
That kept so many warm.

I've heard it in the chillest land,
And on the strangest sea;
Yet, never, in extremity,
It asked a crumb of me.

Emily Dickinson (1830–1886)

Macavity: The Mystery Cat

Macavity's a Mystery Cat: he's called the Hidden Paw—
For he's the master criminal who can defy the Law.
He's the bafflement of Scotland Yard, the Flying Squad's
   despair:
For when they reach the scene of crime—*Macavity's not
   there!*

Macavity, Macavity, there's no one like Macavity,
He's broken every human law, he breaks the law of gravity.
His powers of levitation would make a fakir stare,
And when you reach the scene of crime—*Macavity's not
   there!*
You may seek him in the basement, you may look up in
   the air—
But I tell you once and once again, *Macavity's not there!*

Macavity's a ginger cat, he's very tall and thin;
You would know him if you saw him, for his eyes are
   sunken in.
His brow is deeply lined with thought, his head is highly
   domed;
His coat is dusty from neglect, his whiskers are uncombed.
He sways his head from side to side, with movements like
   a snake;
And when you think he's half asleep, he's always wide
   awake.

Macavity, Macavity, there's no one like Macavity,
For he's a fiend in feline shape, a monster of depravity.
You may meet him in a by-street, you may see him in the
square—
But when a crime's discovered, then *Macavity's not there!*

He's outwardly respectable. (They say he cheats at cards.)
And his footprints are not found in any file of Scotland
Yard's.
And when the larder's looted, or the jewel-case is rifled,
Or when the milk is missing, or another Peke's been
stifled,
Or the greenhouse glass is broken, and the trellis past
repair—
Ay, there's the wonder of the thing! *Macavity's not there!*

And when the Foreign Office find a Treaty's gone astray,
Or the Admiralty lose some plans and drawings by the way,
There may be a scrap of paper in the hall or on the stair—
But it's useless to investigate—*Macavity's not there!*
And when the loss has been disclosed, the Secret Service
say:
'It *must* have been Macavity!'—but he's a mile away.
You'll be sure to find him resting, or a-licking of his
thumbs,
Or engaged in doing complicated long division sums.

Macavity, Macavity, there's no one like Macavity,
There never was a Cat of such deceitfulness and suavity.
He always has an alibi, and one or two to spare:
At whatever time the deed took place—*MACAVITY
 WASN'T THERE!*
And they say that all the Cats whose wicked deeds are
 widely known
(I might mention Mungojerrie, I might mention
 Griddlebone)
Are nothing more than agents for the Cat who all the time
Just controls their operations: the Napoleon of Crime!

T. S. Eliot (1888–1965)

Caledonia

Caledonia! thou land of the mountain and rock,
    Of the ocean, the mist, and the wind—
Thou land of the torrent, the pine, and the oak,
    Of the roebuck, the hart, and the hind;
Though bare are thy cliffs, and though barren thy glens,
    Though bleak thy dun islands appear,
Yet kind are the hearts, and undaunted the clans,
    That roam on these mountains so drear!

A foe from abroad, or a tyrant at home,
    Could never thy ardour restrain;
The marshall'd array of imperial Rome
    Essay'd thy proud spirit in vain!
Firm seat of religion, of valour, of truth,
    Of genius unshackled and free,
The muses have left all the vales of the south,
    My loved Caledonia, for thee!

Sweet land of the bay and wild-winding deeps
    Where loveliness slumbers at even,
While far in the depth of the blue water sleeps
    A calm little motionless heaven!
Thou land of the valley, the moor, and the hill,
    Of the storm and the proud rolling wave—
Yes, thou art the land of fair liberty still,
And the land of my forefathers' grave!

James Hogg (1770–1835)

DECEMBER

Summer Hath His Joys, and Winter His Delights

Piano

Softly, in the dusk, a woman is singing to me;
Taking me back down the vista of years, till I see
A child sitting under the piano, in the boom of the
    tingling strings
And pressing the small, poised feet of a mother who
    smiles as she sings.

In spite of myself, the insidious mastery of song,
Betrays me back, till the heart of one weeps to belong,
To the old Sunday evenings at home, with winter outside
And hymns in the cosy parlour, the tinkling piano our
    guide.

So now it is vain for the singer to burst into clamour
With the great black piano appassionato. The glamour
Of childish days is upon me, my manhood is cast
Down in the flood of remembrance, I weep like a child
    for the past.

D. H. Lawrence (1885–1930)

Now Winter Nights Enlarge

Now winter nights enlarge
  The number of their hours;
And clouds their storms discharge
  Upon the airy towers.
Let now the chimneys blaze
  And cups o'erflow with wine,
Let well-turned words amaze
  With harmony divine.
Now yellow waxen lights
  Shall wait on honey love
While youthful revels, masques, and courtly sights
  Sleep's leaden spells remove.

This time doth well dispense
  With lovers' long discourse;
Much speech hath some defense,
  Though beauty no remorse.
All do not all things well;
  Some measures comely tread,
Some knotted riddles tell,
  Some poems smoothly read.
The summer hath his joys,
  And winter his delights;
Though love and all his pleasures are but toys,
  They shorten tedious nights.

Thomas Campion (1567–1620)

Winter-Time

Late lies the wintry sun a-bed,
A frosty, fiery sleepy-head;
Blinks but an hour or two; and then,
A blood-red orange, sets again.

Before the stars have left the skies,
At morning in the dark I rise;
And shivering in my nakedness,
By the cold candle, bathe and dress.

Close by the jolly fire I sit
To warm my frozen bones a bit;
Or with a reindeer-sled, explore
The colder countries round the door.

When to go out, my nurse doth wrap
Me in my comforter and cap:
The cold wind burns my face, and blows
Its frosty pepper up my nose.

Black are my steps on silver sod;
Thick blows my frosty breath abroad;
And tree and house, and hill and lake,
Are frosted like a wedding-cake.

Robert Louis Stevenson (1850–1894)

The Call

From our low seat beside the fire
Where we have dozed and dreamed and watched
  the glow
Or raked the ashes, stopping so
We scarcely saw the sun or rain
Above, or looked much higher
Than this same quiet red or burned-out fire.
To-night we heard a call,
A rattle on the window-pane,
A voice on the sharp air,
And felt a breath stirring our hair,
A flame within us: Something swift and tall
Swept in and out and that was all.
Was it a bright or a dark angel? Who can know?
It left no mark upon the snow,
But suddenly it snapped the chain
Unbarred, flung wide the door
Which will not shut again;
And so we cannot sit here any more.
We must arise and go:
The world is cold without
And dark and hedged about
With mystery and enmity and doubt,
But we must go
Though yet we do not know
Who called, or what marks we shall leave upon the snow.

Charlotte Mew (1869–1928)

Time's wingèd chariot

FROM *TO HIS COY MISTRESS*

But at my back I always hear
Time's wingèd chariot hurrying near:
And yonder all before us lie
Deserts of vast eternity.
Thy beauty shall no more be found;
Nor, in thy marble vault, shall sound
My echoing song.

Andrew Marvell (1621–1678)

Anthem for Doomed Youth

What passing-bells for these who die as cattle?
  Only the monstrous anger of the guns.
  Only the stuttering rifles' rapid rattle
Can patter out their hasty orisons.
No mockeries now for them; no prayers nor bells,
  Nor any voice of mourning save the choirs,—
The shrill, demented choirs of wailing shells;
  And bugles calling for them from sad shires.

What candles may be held to speed them all?
  Not in the hands of boys, but in their eyes
Shall shine the holy glimmers of goodbyes.
  The pallor of girls' brows shall be their pall;
Their flowers the tenderness of patient minds,
And each slow dusk a drawing-down of blinds.

Wilfred Owen (1893–1918)

The splendour falls on castle walls

FROM *THE PRINCESS*

The splendour falls on castle walls
    And snowy summits old in story:
  The long light shakes across the lakes,
    And the wild cataract leaps in glory.
Blow, bugle, blow, set the wild echoes flying,
Blow, bugle; answer, echoes, dying, dying, dying.

  O hark, O hear! how thin and clear,
    And thinner, clearer, farther going!
  O sweet and far from cliff and scar
    The horns of Elfland faintly blowing!
Blow, let us hear the purple glens replying:
Blow, bugle; answer, echoes, dying, dying, dying.

  O love, they die in yon rich sky,
    They faint on hill or field or river:
  Our echoes roll from soul to soul,
    And grow for ever and for ever.
Blow, bugle, blow, set the wild echoes flying,
And answer, echoes, answer, dying, dying, dying.

Alfred, Lord Tennyson (1809–1892)

Do not go gentle into that good night

Do not go gentle into that good night,
Old age should burn and rave at close of day;
Rage, rage against the dying of the light.

Though wise men at their end know dark is right,
Because their words had forked no lightning they
Do not go gentle into that good night.

Good men, the last wave by, crying how bright
Their frail deeds might have danced in a green bay,
Rage, rage against the dying of the light.

Wild men who caught and sang the sun in flight,
And learn, too late, they grieved it on its way,
Do not go gentle into that good night.

Grave men, near death, who see with blinding sight
Blind eyes could blaze like meteors and be gay,
Rage, rage against the dying of the light.

And you, my father, there on the sad height,
Curse, bless, me now with your fierce tears, I pray.
Do not go gentle into that good night.
Rage, rage against the dying of the light.

Dylan Thomas (1914–1953)

Compensation

I should be glad of loneliness
And hours that go on broken wings,
A thirsty body, a tired heart
And the unchanging ache of things,
If I could make a single song
As lovely and as full of light,
As hushed and brief as a falling star
On a winter night.

Sara Teasdale (1884–1933)

Indolence

I praise the tender flower,
That on a mournful day
Bloomed in my garden bower
And made the winter gay.
Its loveliness contented
My heart tormented.

I praise the gentle maid
Whose happy voice and smile
To confidence betrayed
My doleful heart awhile:
And gave my spirit deploring
Fresh wings for soaring.

The maid for very fear
Of love I durst not tell:
The rose could never hear,
Though I bespake her well:
So in my song I bind them
For all to find them.

Robert Bridges (1844–1930)

The Oak

Live thy Life,
   Young and old,
Like yon oak,
Bright in spring,
   Living gold;

Summer-rich
   Then; and then
Autumn-changed
Soberer-hued
   Gold again.

All his leaves
   Fallen at length,
Look, he stands,
Trunk and bough
   Naked strength.

Alfred, Lord Tennyson (1809–1892)

The Corn-Stalk Fiddle

When the corn's all cut and the bright stalks shine
  Like the burnished spears of a field of gold;
When the field-mice rich on the nubbins dine,
  And the frost comes white and the wind blows cold;
Then its heigho fellows and hi-diddle-diddle,
For the time is ripe for the corn-stalk fiddle.

And you take a stalk that is straight and long,
  With an expert eye to its worthy points,
And you think of the bubbling strains of song
  That are bound between its pithy joints—
Then you cut out strings, with a bridge in the middle,
With a corn-stalk bow for a corn-stalk fiddle.

Then the strains that grow as you draw the bow
  O'er the yielding strings with a practiced hand!
And the music's flow never loud but low
  Is the concert note of a fairy band.
Oh, your dainty songs are a misty riddle
To the simple sweets of the corn-stalk fiddle.

When the eve comes on and our work is done
  And the sun drops down with a tender glance,
With their hearts all prime for the harmless fun,
  Come the neighbor girls for the evening's dance,
And they wait for the well-known twist and twiddle,
More time than tune—from the corn-stalk fiddle.

Then brother Jabez takes the bow,
    While Ned stands off with Susan Bland,
Then Henry stops by Milly Snow
    And John takes Nellie Jones's hand,
While I pair off with Mandy Biddle,
And scrape, scrape, scrape goes the corn-stalk fiddle.

'Salute your partners,' comes the call,
    'All join hands and circle round,'
'Grand train back,' and 'Balance all,'
    Footsteps lightly spurn the ground,
'Take your lady and balance down the middle'
To the merry strains of the corn-stalk fiddle.

So the night goes on and the dance is o'er,
    And the merry girls are homeward gone,
But I see it all in my sleep once more,
    And I dream till the very break of dawn
Of an impish dance on a red-hot griddle
To the screech and scrape of a corn-stalk fiddle.

Paul Laurence Dunbar (1872–1906)

When icicles hang by the wall

FROM *LOVE'S LABOUR'S LOST*, ACT V, SCENE II

When icicles hang by the wall,
   And Dick the shepherd blows his nail,
And Tom bears logs into the hall,
   And milk comes frozen home in pail,
When blood is nipped, and ways be foul,
Then nightly sings the staring owl,
     To-whoo;
To-whit, to-whoo, a merry note,
While greasy Joan doth keel the pot.

When all aloud the wind doth blow,
   And coughing drowns the parson's saw,
And birds sit brooding in the snow,
   And Marian's nose looks red and raw,
When roasted crabs hiss in the bowl,
Then nightly sings the staring owl,
     To-whoo;
To-whit, to-whoo, a merry note,
While greasy Joan doth keel the pot.

William Shakespeare (1564–1616)

This is the charm of poetry

FROM THE NOVEL *ETHEL CHURCHILL*

This is the charm of poetry: it comes
On sad perturbed moments; and its thoughts,
Like pearls amid the troubled waters, gleam.
That which we garnered in our eager youth,
Becomes a long delight in after years:
The mind is strengthened, and the heart refreshed
By some old memory of gifted words,
That bring sweet feelings, answering to our own,
Or dreams that waken some more lofty mood
Than dwelleth with the commonplace of life.

L. E. L. (Elizabeth Letitia Landon) (1802–1838)

The secret ministry of frost

FROM *FROST AT MIDNIGHT*

... all seasons shall be sweet to thee,
Whether the summer clothe the general earth
With greenness, or the redbreast sit and sing
Betwixt the tufts of snow on the bare branch
Of mossy apple tree, while the night thatch
Smokes in the sun-thaw; whether the eave-drops fall
Heard only in the trances of the blast,
Or if the secret ministry of frost
Shall hang them up in silent icicles,
Quietly shining to the quiet Moon.

Samuel Taylor Coleridge (1772–1834)

Like birds from the lonely land of snow

FROM *FRUIT-GATHERING*

Your speech is simple, my Master, but not theirs who
    talk of you.
I understand the voice of your stars and the silence of
    your trees.
I know that my heart would open like a flower; that my
    life has filled itself at a hidden fountain.
Your songs, like birds from the lonely land of snow,
    are winging to build their nests in my heart against the
    warmth of its April, and I am content to wait for the
    merry season.

Rabindranath Tagore (1861–1941)
Translated from the Bengali by the author

Ask Me

Some time when the river is ice ask me
mistakes I have made. Ask me whether
what I have done is my life. Others
have come in their slow way into
my thought, and some have tried to help
or to hurt: ask me what difference
their strongest love or hate has made.

I will listen to what you say.
You and I can turn and look
at the silent river and wait. We know
the current is there, hidden; and there
are comings and goings from miles away
that hold the stillness exactly before us.
What the river says, that is what I say.

William Stafford (1914–1993)

Silver

Slowly, silently, now the moon
Walks the night in her silver shoon;
This way, and that, she peers, and sees
Silver fruit upon silver trees;
One by one the casements catch
Her beams beneath the silvery thatch;
Couched in his kennel, like a log,
With paws of silver sleeps the dog;
From their shadowy cote the white breasts peep
Of doves in a silver-feathered sleep;
A harvest mouse goes scampering by,
With silver claws, and silver eye;
And moveless fish in the water gleam,
By silver reeds in a silver stream.

Walter de la Mare (1873–1956)

The ice was here, the ice was there

FROM *THE RIME OF THE ANCIENT MARINER*, PART I

And now there came both mist and snow,
And it grew wondrous cold:
And ice, mast-high, came floating by,
As green as emerald.

And through the drifts the snowy clifts
Did send a dismal sheen:
Nor shapes of men nor beasts we ken—
The ice was all between.

The ice was here, the ice was there,
The ice was all around:
It cracked and growled, and roared and howled,
Like noises in a swound!

Samuel Taylor Coleridge (1772–1834)

What should we speak of when we are old as you?

FROM *CYMBELINE*, ACT III, SCENE III

What should we speak of
When we are old as you? When we shall hear
The rain and wind beat dark December, how,
In this our pinching cave, shall we discourse
The freezing hours away? We have seen nothing;
We are beastly, subtle as the fox for prey,
Like warlike as the wolf for what we eat;
Our valour is to chase what flies; our cage
We make a choir, as doth the prison'd bird,
And sing our bondage freely.

William Shakespeare (1564–1616)

Ode to Winter

We hoard light, hunkered in holt and burrow,
in cave, *cwtsh*, den, earth, hut, lair.
Sun blinks. Trees take down their hair.
Dusk wipes horizons, seeps into the room,
the last flame of geranium in the gloom.

In the shortening day, bring in the late flowers
to crisp in a vase, beech to break into leaf,
a branch of lark. Take winter by the throat.
Feed the common birds, tits and finches,
the spotted woodpecker in his opera coat.

Let's learn to love the icy winter moon,
or moonless dark and winter constellations,
Jupiter's glow, a slow, incoming plane,
neighbourly windows, someone's flickering screen,
a lamp-lit page, drawn curtains.

Let us praise intimacy, talk and books,
music and silence, wind and rain,
the beautiful bones of trees, taste of cold air,
darkening fields, the glittering city,
that winter longing, *hiraeth*, something like prayer.

Under the stilled heartbeat of trees,
wind-snapped branches, mulch and root,
a million bluebell bulbs lie low
ready to flare in lengthening light,
after the dark, the frozen earth, the snow.

Out there, fox and buzzard, kite and crow
are clearing the ground for the myth.
On the darkest day bring in the tree,
cool and pungent as forest. Turn up the music.
Pour us a glass. Dress the house in pagan finery.

Gillian Clarke (b.1937)

The Sugar-Plum Tree

Have you ever heard of the Sugar-Plum Tree?
  'Tis a marvel of great renown!
It blooms on the shore of the Lollypop sea
  In the garden of Shut-Eye Town;
The fruit that it bears is so wondrously sweet
  (As those who have tasted it say)
That good little children have only to eat
  Of that fruit to be happy next day.

When you've got to the tree, you would have a hard time
  To capture the fruit which I sing;
The tree is so tall that no person could climb
  To the boughs where the sugar-plums swing!
But up in that tree sits a chocolate cat,
  And a gingerbread dog prowls below;
And this is the way you contrive to get at
  Those sugar-plums tempting you so:

You say but the word to that gingerbread dog
  And he barks with such terrible zest
That the chocolate cat is at once all agog,
  As her swelling proportions attest.
And the chocolate cat goes cavorting around
  From *this* leafy limb unto *that,*
And the sugar-plums tumble, of course, to the ground—
  Hurrah for that chocolate cat!

There are marshmallows, gumdrops, and peppermint canes,
    With stripings of scarlet or gold,
And you carry away of the treasure that rains,
    As much as your apron can hold!
So come, little child, cuddle closer to me
    In your dainty white nightcap and gown,
And I'll rock you away to that Sugar-Plum Tree
    In the garden of Shut-Eye Town.

Eugene Field (1850–1895)

Love and Friendship

Love is like the wild rose-briar;
　Friendship like the holly-tree.
The holly is dark when the rose-briar blooms
　But which will bloom most constantly?

The wild rose-briar is sweet in spring,
　Its summer blossoms scent the air;
Yet wait till winter comes again
　And who will call the wild-briar fair?

Then scorn the silly rose-wreath now
　And deck thee with the holly's sheen,
That when December blights thy brow
　He still may leave thy garland green.

Emily Brontë (1818–1848)

Christmas Landscape

Tonight the wind gnaws
with teeth of glass,
the jackdaw shivers
in caged branches of iron,
the stars have talons.

There is hunger in the mouth
of vole and badger,
silver agonies of breath
in the nostril of the fox,
ice on the rabbit's paw.

Tonight has no moon,
no food for the pilgrim;
the fruit tree is bare,
the rose bush a thorn
and the ground is bitter with stones.

But the mole sleeps, and the hedgehog
lies curled in a womb of leaves,
the bean and the wheat-seed
hug their germs in the earth
and the stream moves under the ice.

Tonight there is no moon,
but a new star opens
like a silver trumpet over the dead.
tonight in a nest of ruins
the blessèd babe is laid.

And the fir tree warms to a bloom of candles,
and the child lights his lantern,
stares at his tinselled toy;
our hearts and hearths
smoulder with live ashes.

In the blood of our grief
the cold earth is suckled,
in our agony the womb
convulses its seed,
in the first cry of anguish
the child's first breath is born.

Laurie Lee (1914–1997)

Hymn to the Belly

FROM *PLEASURE RECONCIL'D TO VERTUE*

Room! room! make room for the Bouncing Belly,
First father of sauce, and deviser of jelly;
Prime master of arts, and the giver of wit,
That found out the excellent engine, the spit;
The plough, and the flail, the mill and the hopper,
The hutch and the boulter, the furnace and copper,
The oven, the bavin, the mawkin, the peel,
The hearth and the range, the dog and the wheel:
He, he first invented the hogshead and tun,
The gimlet and vice too, and taught them to run,
And since, with the funnel an Hippocras bag,
He has made of himself, that now he cries swag!
Which shows, though the pleasure be but of four inches,
Yet he is a weasel, the gullet that pinches
Of any delight, and not spares from his back
Whatever to make of the belly a sack!
Hail, hail, plump paunch! O the founder of taste,
For fresh meats, or powder'd, or pickle, or paste,
Devourer of broil'd, baked, roasted or sod;
And emptier of cups, be they even or odd.
All which have now made thee so wide in the waist,
As scarce with no pudding thou art to be laced;
But eating and drinking until thou dost nod,
Thou break'st all thy girdles, and break'st forth a god.

Ben Jonson (1572–1637)

There was a boy

FROM *THE PRELUDE* (1805), BOOK V

There was a boy: ye knew him well, ye cliffs
And islands of Winander!—many a time
At evening, when the earliest stars began
To move along the edges of the hills,
Rising or setting, would he stand alone
Beneath the trees or by the glimmering lake,
And there, with fingers interwoven, both hands
Pressed closely palm to palm, and to his mouth
Uplifted, he, as through an instrument,
Blew mimic hootings to the silent owls,
That they might answer him; and they would shout
Across the watery vale, and shout again,
Responsive to his call, with quivering peals,
And long halloos and screams, and echoes loud,
Redoubled and redoubled, concourse wild
Of jocund din; and, when a lengthened pause
Of silence came and baffled his best skill,
Then sometimes, in that silence while he hung
Listening, a gentle shock of mild surprise
Has carried far into his heart the voice
Of mountain torrents; or the visible scene
Would enter unawares into his mind,
With all its solemn imagery, its rocks,
Its woods, and that uncertain heaven, received
Into the bosom of the steady lake.

William Wordsworth (1770–1850)

His Poetry His Pillar

Only a little more
I have to write:
Then I'll give o'er,
And bid the world good-night.

'Tis but a flying minute,
That I must stay,
Or linger in it:
And then I must away.

O Time, that cut'st down all,
And scarce leav'st here
Memorial
Of any men that were;

—How many lie forgot
In vaults beneath,
And piece-meal rot
Without a fame in death?

Behold this living stone
I rear for me,
Ne'er to be thrown
Down, envious Time, by thee.

Pillars let some set up
If so they please;
Here is my hope,
And my Pyramides.

Robert Herrick (1591–1674)

The Darkling Thrush

I leant upon a coppice gate
　When Frost was spectre-gray,
And Winter's dregs made desolate
　The weakening eye of day.
The tangled bine-stems scored the sky
　Like strings of broken lyres,
And all mankind that haunted nigh
　Had sought their household fires.

The land's sharp features seemed to be
　The Century's corpse outleant,
His crypt the cloudy canopy,
　The wind his death-lament.
The ancient pulse of germ and birth
　Was shrunken hard and dry,
And every spirit upon earth
　Seemed fervourless as I.

At once a voice arose among
　The bleak twigs overhead
In a full-hearted evensong
　Of joy illimited;
An aged thrush, frail, gaunt, and small,
　In blast-beruffled plume,
Had chosen thus to fling his soul
　Upon the growing gloom.

So little cause for carolings
  Of such ecstatic sound
Was written on terrestrial things
  Afar or nigh around,
That I could think there trembled through
  His happy good-night air
Some blessed Hope, whereof he knew
  And I was unaware.

Thomas Hardy (1840–1928)

Lines Composed in a
Wood on a Windy Day

My soul is awakened, my spirit is soaring
And carried aloft on the wings of the breeze;
For above and around me the wild wind is roaring,
Arousing to rapture the earth and the seas.

The long withered grass in the sunshine is glancing,
The bare trees are tossing their branches on high;
The dead leaves beneath them are merrily dancing,
The white clouds are scudding across the blue sky

I wish I could see how the ocean is lashing
The foam of its billows to whirlwinds of spray;
I wish I could see how its proud waves are dashing,
And hear the wild roar of their thunder to-day!

Anne Brontë (1820–1849)

Midnight never come

FROM *DOCTOR FAUSTUS*, ACT V, SCENE II

Stand still, you ever-moving spheres of heaven,
That time may cease, and midnight never come;
Fair Nature's eye, rise, rise again, and make
Perpetual day; or let this hour be but
A year, a month, a week, a natural day,
That Faustus may repent and save his soul!
O lente, lente currite, noctis equi!
The stars move still, time runs, the clock will strike ...

Christopher Marlowe (1564–1593)

Ring Out, Wild Bells

FROM *IN MEMORIAM A.H.H.*

Ring out, wild bells, to the wild sky,
  The flying cloud, the frosty light:
  The year is dying in the night;
Ring out, wild bells, and let him die.

Ring out the old, ring in the new,
  Ring, happy bells, across the snow:
  The year is going, let him go;
Ring out the false, ring in the true.

Ring out the grief that saps the mind
  For those that here we see no more;
  Ring out the feud of rich and poor,
Ring in redress to all mankind.

Ring out a slowly dying cause,
  And ancient forms of party strife;
  Ring in the nobler modes of life,
With sweeter manners, purer laws.

Ring out the want, the care, the sin,
  The faithless coldness of the times;
  Ring out, ring out my mournful rhymes
But ring the fuller minstrel in.

Alfred, Lord Tennyson (1809–1892)

Index of First Lines

And wilt thou leave me thus 35
As from the house your mother sees 129
As I walked out one morning in the springtime of the
      year 138–9
As we come marching, marching, in the beauty of the
      day 89–90
At the mid hour of night, when stars are weeping, I fly
      177
At the top of the house the apples are laid in rows 320
Away! Away! We will sail the sea 75

Be not afeard. The isle is full of noises 240
Begin again to the summoning birds 339
Behold the apples' rounded worlds 307
Betty Botta bought some butter 142
Between the showers I went my way 96
Black grows the southern sky betokening rain 108
Break, break, break 393
But at my back I always hear 420
But silent musings urge the mind to seek 109
But then there comes that moment rare 196

Caledonia! thou land of the mountain and rock 412
Cauld blaws the wind frae east to west 36
Clear and cool, clear and cool 147
Come live with me and be my love 156
Come, read to me some poem 50
Come when the nights are bright with stars 25

Daphnis dearest, wherefore weave me 125
Dark the night, with breath all flowers 362
Dawn talks to Day 158
Did you too see it, drifting, all night, on the black river? 345
Do not go gentle into that good night 423
Do you ask what the birds say? The Sparrow, the Dove
      160

453

Index of Poets

Sources

W. H. Auden, 'Funeral Blues', copyright © 1940 by W. H. Auden. Reprinted by permission of Curtis Brown, Ltd. All rights reserved (UK). 'Funeral Blues', copyright 1940, © renewed 1968 by W. H. Auden; from COLLECTED POEMS by W. H. Auden, edited by Edward Mendelson. Used by permission of Random House, an imprint and division of Penguin Random House LLC. All rights reserved (US).

W. H. Auden, 'Night Mail' Copyright © 1938 by W. H. Auden. Reprinted by permission of Curtis Brown, Ltd. All rights reserved (UK). 'Night Mail', copyright 1938, © renewed 1966 by W. H. Auden; from COLLECTED POEMS by W. H. Auden, edited by Edward Mendelson. Used by permission of Random House, an imprint and division of Penguin Random House LLC. All rights reserved (US).

Maya Angelou, 'Still I Rise' from AND STILL I RISE: A BOOK OF POEMS by Maya Angelou, copyright © 1978 by Maya Angelou. Used by permission of Random House, an imprint and division of Penguin Random House LLC. All rights reserved.

Wendell Berry, 'The Peace of Wild Things' from *The Peace of Wild Things*, Penguin, 2018. © Wendell Berry/Penguin Random House/Abner Stein Ltd.

Elizabeth Bishop, 'One Art', © The Estate of Elizabeth Bishop, Penguin Random House Ltd.

Gwendolyn Brooks, 'Speech to the Young: Speech to the Progress-Toward (Among them Nora and Henry III)' reprinted by consent of Brooks Permissions.

Farjeon, Eleanor, 'The Distance' from *Silver, Sand and Snow*, Macmillan Children's Books, 2000. Reproduced by permission of David Higham Associates.

Hafiz (trans. Daniel Ladinsky), 'All the Hemispheres', from the Penguin publication *The Subject Tonight is Love: 60 Wild and Sweet Poems of Hafiz* by Daniel Ladinsky, © 2003 and used with permission. www.danielladinsky.com.

Joy Harjo, 'Remember', copyright © 1983 by Joy Harjo, from SHE HAD SOME HORSES by Joy Harjo. Used by permission of W. W. Norton & Company, Inc.

Robert Hayden, 'Those Winter Sundays', copyright © 1966 by Robert Hayden, from COLLECTED POEMS OF ROBERT HAYDEN by Robert Hayden, edited by Frederick Glaysher. Used by permission of Liveright Publishing Corporation.

Langston Hughes, 'Mother to Son', from *African-American Poetry: An Anthology 1773–1927*, published by Dover Books, 1997. Reproduced by permission of David Higham Associates.

Brendan Kennelly, 'Begin', from *Familiar Strangers: New and Selected Poems 1960–2004*, published by Bloodaxe Books, 2004. Reprinted with permission of Bloodaxe Books.

Lotte Kramer, 'The Tablecloth', from *More New and Collected Poems* by Lotte Kramer (Rockingham Press). Reprinted by permission of Rockingham Press.

Laurie Lee, 'Home from Abroad', reproduced with permission of Curtis Brown Group Ltd, London on behalf of the Beneficiaries of the Estate of Laurie Lee. Copyright © Laurie Lee.

Acknowledgements

A very big thank you to the great team at Batsford, particularly Nicola Newman and Tina Persaud for all that they have done in the making of this anthology.

I am so grateful to The Reader – its staff, volunteers and group members – for showing me the power and application of great literature. Many of these poems have been read aloud and discussed in 'shared reading' groups that I have either led or taken part in while working and volunteering for The Reader.

Thank you to my local library in New Malden, Kingston-upon-Thames and The National Poetry Library at the South Bank as well as The British Library – and the wonderful librarians and library assistants who work there. The web also makes so much poetry easily available and two online resources that have been invaluable are Project Gutenberg at gutenberg.org and the Poetry Foundation at poetryfoundation.org.

Grateful thanks to my family for their support and encouragement.

And finally, to all the poets featured in this collection (especially 'Anon'): reading, enjoying and sharing these poems feels like the best way to honour and thank them.

About the author

Liz Ison studied English literature at Cambridge, before training as a speech and language therapist. She has a doctorate from UCL for research into childhood speech and literacy development. In 2015, after ten years in education research for the UK government, Liz trained with British charity The Reader and has since been running shared reading groups, in person and online.

Dear Reader,

I hope you've enjoyed this anthology.

If you want to find out more about reading aloud, you may be interested in the work of The Reader, a charity that uses the power of literature and reading aloud to transform lives.

The Reader's staff and dedicated volunteers bring people together in small groups to read and talk about great stories and poems together – including some of the poems you'll find in this anthology. We call this Shared Reading. There are Shared Reading groups happening all around the country: in schools, community spaces, care homes. We read with families, with people with physical and mental health conditions, those coping with or recovering from addiction, and people in the criminal justice system.

We always read aloud in our Shared Reading groups. It is part of what makes these groups different from any other book group. Through the act of reading it aloud, the literature becomes alive in the room, and creates a powerful connection between reader and listener. Anyone who was lucky enough to be read to as a child knows that connection – it is relaxing, intimate and creates the warm sense of being cared for. The person reading aloud benefits too as it helps build confidence and the ability to focus, to stay 'in the moment.'

We know that Shared Reading improves wellbeing, reduces isolation and helps people find new meaning in their lives. To find out more about how you could get involved, visit www.thereader.org.uk.

From

Katie Clark, Director of Literature at The Reader

The Reader